Heidegger and Modernity

Luc Ferry and Alain Renaut

Heidegger and Modernity

Translated by Franklin Philip

The University of Chicago Press · Chicago and London

Luc Ferry and Alain Renaut have published several books together, including *La Pensée 68*. Ferry teaches political science at the Sorbonne and at Caen. His *Political Philosophy*, of which the third volume was coauthored by Alain Renaut, is also being published by the University of Chicago Press in Franklin Philip's translation. Renaut, who teaches philosophy at Nantes, is the author of *Le système du droit*.

The University of Chicago Press, Chicago 60637
The University of Chicago Press, Ltd., London
© 1990 by The University of Chicago
All rights reserved. Published 1990
Printed in the United States of America

99 98 97 96 95 94 93 92 91 90   5 4 3 2 1

Library of Congress Cataloging-in-Publication Data

Ferry, Luc.
   [Heidegger et les modernes. English]
   Heidegger and modernity / Luc Ferry and Alain Renaut ; translated by Franklin Philip.
      p. cm.
   Translation of: Heidegger et les modernes.
   Includes bibliographical references.
   ISBN 0-226-24462-8
   1. Heidegger, Martin, 1889–1976—Influence. 2. Philosophy, French—20th century. 3. National socialism. 4. France—Intellectual life—20th century.   I. Renaut, Alain. II. Title.
B3279.H49F43   1990
193—dc20   89-28256
                                                                CIP

Originally published in Paris under the title *Heidegger et les Modernes*, © 1988, Éditions Grasset & Fasquelle.

⊗ The paper used in this publication meets the minimum requirements of the American National Standard for Information Sciences—Permanence of Paper for Printed Library Materials, ANSI Z39.48-1984.

Contents

Introduction

Intellectual history is definitely not a thankless subject. For the unsuspecting, it may have some heady surprises in store. When in 1984 we set about writing a book on contemporary antihumanism,[1] little did we imagine that our hopes, or rather our fears, would be so fully confirmed. Because of the demise of Marxism, our intention was to deconstruct the French variants of Heideggerianism. After spending nearly ten years patiently studying Heidegger together at a seminar of the Collège de Philosophie,[2] we have reached the conviction that his indictment of modern times and humanism, which he saw as going back to Descartes and the philosophes of the Enlightenment, could at the very best lead to a radical criticism of every feature of the democratic world: the world of technology and mass culture, of course, but also the world of human rights and, more generally, the program of resolving through public discussion the questions constantly posed by the contemporary dynamics of a continual break with tradition.

So we were not speaking lightly when we used the term "antihumanism" to refer to the philosophical thematization of this rejection of modernity which, whether hostile or anguished, often unjust, sometimes legitimate, was always done from a viewpoint of radical exteriority from which any compromise with modernity was seen as a compromise with one's conscience.

Is Nazism a Humanism?

Faced with the question of Heidegger's Nazism, the "French Heideggerians" gathered around Jacques Derrida have irrevocably chosen their side and found their concept through an extraordinary recommendation: if Heidegger was a Nazi, which no one now can dispute, it certainly was not because he condemned the world of democratic humanism and thus saw the appeal of a conservative revolution; and if, as one student of Derrida's coolly asserts, "Nazism is a humanism" (*sic*),[3] we should judge that the Heidegger of 1933 was naturally led to Nazism because he was still in the grip of a humanistic and spiritualistic tradition he had not yet adequately deconstructed, Q.E.D.

The wording of this claim is slightly ridiculous, for it stems from a polemic against our own book. For us, the time for polemics is past; resisting the temptation to deride, we think it more fruitful to indicate at the outset just what this claim basically means and how in its way it typifies not just a philosophical error but perhaps *the* error par excellence of contemporary French philosophy.

Listen to Philippe Lacoue-Labarthe:

> Nazism is a humanism in that it rests on a determination of *humanitas*, which is, in its eyes, more powerful, i.e., more effective, than any other. The subject of absolute self-creation, even if it transcends all the determinations of the modern subject in an immediately natural position (the particularity of race), brings together and concretizes these same determinations (as does Stalinism with the subject of absolute self-production) and sets itself up as *the* subject, absolutely speaking. The fact that this subject lacks the universality that seems to define the *humanitas* of humanism in the usual sense does not, however, make Nazism an antihu-

manism. Quite simply, it fits Nazism into the logic, of which there are many other examples, of the realization and concretization of "abstractions."

By means of a double slippage in the meaning of humanism, the meaning of these remarks is clear:

To arrive at the absurd conclusion that Nazism is a humanism (in passing, must we now forget Sartre, who entitled one of his best-known lectures "Existentialism is a Humanism" so that these opinions do not offend the spirit of the times?), we first need to assume that humanism reduces to the wish to give man a definition that assigns to him some *essence* or *nature*.

Next, in a second usurpation, it is necessary to deny any intrinsic difference between a definition of man that tends toward universality and a racial definition that quite explicitly separates man from man.

Thanks to these two maneuvers, we can easily see how Nazism can be a humanism: by splitting humanity into the authentic and the inauthentic, into the properly human (Aryan) and the improperly human (Jewish), Nazism—*because in this sense it is a humanism*—includes a provision for extermination. Thus, because it claimed to identify *the distinguishing feature of man*, "Nazi humanism" sacrificed the nonman to man, and in this way it fits into the logic of modern times launched by Descartes's cogito, the prototypical essentialistic definition of man. True anti-Nazism then would not imply a call for human rights, which are, as Derrida never ceases to remind us, inevitably subject to "terrifying contaminations,"[4] but for a more radical deconstruction of humanism and modernity than the partial deconstruction that enabled Heidegger to be a Nazi.

We would applaud the virtuosity of this turnabout if the question were not so serious. The purpose of this book is not to rehash the trial of Heidegger but to set forth the philosophical meaning of what today is understood as humanism, so that this reductive view of our relation to modernity will clearly appear for what it is.

Two claims need to be justified:

1. Contrary to the claims of contemporary antihumanism, Sartre's definition of humanism, which he was unfortunately to recant, means the denial of a human essence, the refusal to shackle man with some historical or natural definition. In a tradition going back to Rousseau, *man appears as the lone being for whom neither history nor nature can supply codes:* if man has a distinguishing feature, an authenticity (*Eigentlichkeit*), it can only lie in his ability (small difference whether we call it transcendence or freedom) to wrench himself free from every attribution of an essence. In short, if the notion of humanism has a meaning, it is that the distinguishing feature of man is his not having one; the definition of man is to be indefinable; his essence is to have no essence. Things and no doubt animals too are what they are; man alone is nothing: it is impossible for him, without foundering in "bad faith," to equate himself with any identity whatever, whether natural, familial, or social. And although it follows that existentialism is a humanism, authentic humanism is also necessarily an existentialism, for man's existence (eksistence = transcendence, the ability to wrench oneself free of codes) is always beyond any reduction to an essence.

2. We therefore come up against the question of the universal, about which we would be making an understatement if we said that it is rash to dismiss the idea in half a sentence: why can't we see that in authentic humanism the universal does not mean some norm, whatever it might be, in the name of which violence is done to the particular, or for the sake of which particulars are excluded in practice, even exterminated? In this case, reference to the universal means that any "distinguishing feature of man" must belong to all men (the reason why

racism can never be a humanism); but it also means that if this distinguishing property is nothing or freedom, if it is the ability to wrench free of multiple codes that constantly threaten to imprison individuals, the idea of universality is the horizon within which this wrenching occurs. Plainly, each person endlessly risks confusing himself with *particular* determinations; he may *conceive* of himself as belonging to a particular nation, a sex, an ethnic or other group, a role, a social function; thus he may be "a nationalist," "a sexist," "a racist," "a corporatist"—but he may also (and this is the *humanitas* of man) transcend these definitions *by entering into communication with others* (universality).

Thus, it is because man is "a nothingness," and because this nothingness points to universality (communication with others), in short: it is because he is also an *abstract universal* that he can distance himself from particular determinations. The particularity of any definition and, with all the more reason, of a racial definition thus never has the truth of an abstract universal; on the contrary, it is only through abstract universality that we can get away from all the particularisms whose absolutization in the form of a *false universal* leads to the plan of exclusion and even extermination.

It must be said and said again: the two defining elements of humanism are indissolubly linked. To assert that the distinguishing feature of man is his nothingness is to contend that he can wrench free of any particularism (and aim toward universality). Saying that man aims at the universal means that he is a nothingness, that he never wholly confuses himself with any *particular* identity or *being*. The problematic of communication with others, of intersubjectivity, thus proves inseparable from that of humanism as existentialism.

Why under these circumstances do the French Heideggerians need to maintain at any cost—at the cost of truly mind-boggling contortions of the intellect and manipula-

tions of the history of philosophy—the idea that humanism must be the bearer of all ills, even to the point of
being responsible for Heidegger's political deviation?
What imperative needs does Heidegger's thinking meet so
that, to safeguard its purity, we are asked to condemn it for
what it is not (a humanism) rather than for what it is (a
deconstruction of humanism)? From this point of view,
the considerable scandal provoked by Victor Farias's 1987
book, *Heidegger and Nazism*, represents a stunning revelation:[5] faced with this most recent flare-up of a lingering
controversy, we are forced to wonder what makes Heidegger's ideas so indispensable for a large part of the French
intelligentsia, for the debate reopened by Farias has become so widespread that we need to see how unprecedented it is.

From the Heidegger Case to the Farias Affair

"The case of Heidegger is too complex for me to set forth
here." The author of this prudent and dilatory statement
is Sartre. It appeared in 1960 in the opening chapter of his
Critique of Dialectical Reason.[6] Arguing that "any philosophy is practical," Sartre considers what sort of "social
and political weapon" philosophy can supply, and considers its capacity for legitimizing "criticism" "an immediate response by the oppressed to oppression."

Nearly thirty years have passed. The "Heidegger case"
is still just as "complex,"[7] but what person inquiring
about the impact of intellectual activity would still think
of putting off the examination of Heidegger's Nazism?
Several months after its publication, Farias's book continues to fuel a debate of awesome dimensions. The press
teems with position taking, and rare are those who dodge
what is becoming a mandatory exercise. Pierre Aubenque,
Jean Baudrillard, Maurice Blanchot, Pierre Bourdieu,
Michel Deguy, Jacques Derrida, François Fédier, Alain
Finkielkraut, Gérard Granel, Philippe Lacoue-Labarthe,

Emmanuel Lévinas, Stephan Moses, and many others, we among them, have already capitulated, and the end of the phenomenon is not yet in sight. Certainly not on French television, which, calling up André Comte-Sponville, Jean Pierre Faye, François Fédier, and André Glucksmann, has devoted an uncommonly large amount of air time to a controversy that is still remote from the concerns of the general public.[8] The number and variety of commentaries have reached the point that in a few years from now the complete dossier of them will probably represent an excellent and almost "life-sized" survey of the "opinion" of French intellectuals in the late 1980s on questions raised by the political involvements of one of the greatest philosophers of the century.

Why this sudden and sustained interest in half-century-old facts that sparked a lively controversy just after the liberation of France, but that by the 1960s were of interest only to Heidegger specialists? The first debate, from 1945 to 1948, took place in the pages of the journal *Temps modernes*;[9] the debate scarcely mentioned the facts about the personal involvement of the rector of Freiburg University but dealt mainly, and rather abstractly, with the problem of how Heidegger's ideas were related to the advent of Nazism.[10] For lack of an exact assessment of the facts, the discussion remained formal and abruptly ceased. A second controversy, this time concentrated in the journal *Critique*, arose in France from a first attempt to come up with some genuine material for discussion:[11] in 1961 Jean Pierre Faye published a partial translation of the speeches and proclamations from the period of the rectorate.[12] This, however, stirred only the "Heideggerians" of strict obedience, most of them disciples of Jean Beaufret, enthroned since 1946 by the envoi of the "Letter on Humanism" as Heidegger's "official" interlocutor and chargé d'affaires: in 1966, François Fédier, Beaufret's student and right-hand man, alerted by developments in German treatments of texts from the same period,[13] published an article that contented itself with mentioning certain facts strictly confined to the rectorate;[14] Faye replied by raising the problem of Heidegger's attitude after 1934;[15] then the controversy, centering on the translation of Heidegger's use of the adjective *völkisch* ("popular," "national," "racial"?) ceased with a new reply from Fédier.[16] This debate obviously did not go beyond the rather narrow circle of specialists, some in Nazi ideology,[17] others in Heidegger: quite plainly, French intellectuals, at least most of them, like Sartre in 1960, could still judge the question of Heidegger's Nazism to be certainly complex and even important, but did not feel obliged to take sides in a quarrel they felt did not concern them.

Why, in light of Farias's book, is it different today with this third French debate on the "Heidegger case"? The very style of Farias's book, that of an investigation, definitely accounts for some measure of its success. Here, public attention stemmed from many sources, not the least of them curiosity about the underside of history, even if only the history of thought. But it would be simplistic to reduce the repercussions of the text to be the effects of a scandal. What we need to understand is why such a large number of French intellectuals, not just the coterie of Beaufret's disciples, felt themselves touched by the scandal and were unwilling to admit that Heidegger's compromise by Nazism was as extensive as Farias revealed or had the meaning that Farias gave it by forging indissoluble links between the thought of Being and the Nazi involvement, links not imputable to a half-year deviation. In this book our intention is to clarify this agitation among French intellectuals and to reveal its logic and significance.

This commotion is not unrelated—as its startled observers in Germany suggest—to the long delay in France in getting hold of a dossier that had long been truncated (Beaufret and his disciples have raised the withholding of documents to a high art) and crudely imparted in bits and pieces.[18] Prepared more than two years ago, the translation of Heidegger's speeches during his rectorate, only recently published by the journal *le Débat*, was put off following François Fédier's intervention on behalf of Heidegger's son and pressure from the latter on Gallimard, publisher of *le Débat* as well as the French translations of Heidegger's books. How, under these circumstances, could Farias's book, which is primarily a repository of facts, produce this "bomb" effect noted by all the commentators?

Just in itself, the explanation by the overlong retention of the dossier cannot, however, completely explain the intensity of the shock wave. More profoundly, the "Farias affair" in our eyes displays an essential dimension of the French intellectual universe, and a clarification of this uproar in the French intelligentsia should afford greater insight into the lines of force (or weakness) that structure this universe. For we cannot understand the unprecedented scandal created by Farias's book or the defensive strategies it inspired in the Heideggerians if we do not see what role has been played in the France of the past forty years by the reference to Heidegger in a criticism of modern times that has seemingly become an inevitable stage in the life of every intellectual.

The Role of the Intellectual and Criticism of the Modern World

Without taking up the much-belabored question of the "role of the intellectual in the city," we should note the structural and historical reasons why intellectuals are obligated to serve a critical function in democratic societies.

Certainly the notion of the intellectual is, as they say, a "gamble": it can be defined only in a system of contrasts that does not a priori allow the rules to be set precisely. One is always the intellectual of someone else, and one always finds someone "more intellectual than thou."

Nonetheless, two characteristics seem to define the typical ideal intellectual: unlike the expert or specialist, the intellectual is a generalist whom journalists, who play the game in which the image of the intellectual is worked out, seek out for consultation on an uncountable number of subjects. For this very reason, the attitude of the intellectual, again in contrast to that of the expert, is not one of scientific neutrality, but one of involvement or *engagement*, which presupposes a critical distancing with regard to positivity. In this sense, Michel Foucault, and perhaps even more so Sartre, exemplified the ideal intellectual. Not only did each of them always adopt a principled critical position vis-à-vis the democratic world, the positivity of their time, but they could also combine the legitimacies of the philosopher, the writer, and the politico-public man whose moral authority, though disputable and disputed, is always acknowledged. To exploit a distinction dear to Max Weber, the intellectual, the involved generalist in contrast to the specialized and neutral expert, always opts for the ethics of conviction over the ethics of responsibility. It is in choosing this ethics of conviction that for many people he or she symbolizes "courage" and "generosity" compared to the presumed cynicism of the ethics of responsibility—which is why "it's better to be wrong with Sartre than right with Raymond Aron"—a slogan that admirably illustrates the values by which the intellectual establishment identifies and legitimizes itself.

Oddly enough, French intellectuals have scarcely taken any note of this paradox: even when the critical intellectual is inclined to adopt an attitude of radical contempt for "institutions," even when he condemns elections as a "snare for simpletons" and the schools as "academies for bosses and cops," thus *seeming* to take a position of radical externality relative to the democratic world, he is nevertheless simply filling out one of its essential dimensions. Rousseau identified the distinguishing property of democratic societies as a critical relation to the law, the norms, and the authorities: at the heart of a democratic society, one that wants to be "self-instituted," if only indirectly through representative institutions, individuals may condemn all the norms—they may condemn norms they did not create because it was not they who created them, hence norms that seem to be imposed from the outside, and they may condemn norms they *did* create because it was they who created and mastered them and they can in principle modify or change them at will. In such a world, the intellectual personifies the authority of the critic and becomes the spokesman for the legitimate exasperations or resentments that the positivity of laws and facts is bound to provoke in us all. This paradox is thus structurally connected to democratic societies, for in adopting a position that seems to be one of radical externality, the intellectual is in fact playing the game of democracy. This paradox is essential, however, for from it we can almost deduce the obligation of criticism, a reason why in a liberal society the hearts of the intelligentsia will inevitably belong to the left and, should the left chance to come to power, will be, if not reduced to silence, at least forced to adopt a new strategy.

Besides this structural ground for criticism, we need to take account of the historical context in order to understand by what curious twists Heidegger's thinking could become one of the chief sources of criticism of the democratic world, to the point that, through a remarkable reversal of situation, the man who was more than a fellow traveler to Nazism became the chief "philosopher of the left" in contemporary France.

We no doubt need to look back to the immediate postwar period to see the connection between the experience of a severe trauma—the demonization of Europe and Western values—and the genesis of plans for radically transforming society and their realization in the thirdworldism and left-wing politics of the 1950s. The messianic character of these plans, which represent a fundamental criticism of the democratic world, reflected the trauma that people became aware of during the postwar period: the "civilized societies," the entire Western world, could justifiably be suspected of having encouraged, or at least not prevented, the great political calamities of Nazism and colonialist imperialism.

The idea of a "dialectics of the philosophes" thus managed to acquire a philosophical legitimacy that it had never had: far from securing man's emancipation, the philosophes changed into their opposites, as universalism took on the face of Eurocentrism, and rationalism that of the irrationalism inherent in a whole world dominated by the irrational reason represented by instrumental or technological reason.

This is the context in which we must assess the importance of French Marxism, which up to the 1960s still appeared, at the cost of a certain blindness, as the only vision of the world that, though European in origin, was free of the taint of compromise with Nazism or colonialism. Otherwise it would be impossible to understand how the Communist Party in France could become, if not the party of the intellectuals, at least an attractive prospect for philosophers who for other reasons would have been inclined to criticize a thinking that reduces man to history, and history to a logical succession of stages headed in the direction of a classless society. Otherwise, it is impossible to understand how the leftists, who were also spurred by criticism of the Soviet and hence communist bureaucracy, could manage this criticism only in variants of a theory they shared with their archenemy. In this context, it was no accident that the true common ground for the various left-wing movements was third-worldism and the struggle against colonial wars waged by countries that, though liberal democracies, at the time necessarily appeared (we now see why) to be constantly threatening to take on the face of fascism.

It was also during this period in French intellectual his-

tory that the structural anthropology of Claude Lévi-
Strauss, which, though it too was philosophically completely alien and even hostile to Marxism, could join with
it in condemning Eurocentrism. Lévi-Strauss vigorously
attacked the teleological view of history in which Marx
remains embroiled and even exposed the necessarily Eurocentrist implications of this teleology, according to
which the most highly developed industrial nations represent the only possible future for primitive societies inevitably viewed as underdeveloped and not as *other* or *different:* the fact remains that the common enemy was seen
as colonialism and that Marxism could combine all the
legitimacies, at the cost of a structuralist revision of its
presuppositions (a revision performed by Louis Althusser), which relieved it of its economic determinism and
the Hegelian cunning of reason.

There is no need to belabor the point: Marxism has
now collapsed. The reasons for this collapse, which is
presently reaching such proportions as to portend the return of a Marx revisited, concern internal mutations in a
French society that, whatever else we may say, has become
much more democratic in the past thirty years and in
1968 witnessed the emergence of a new political force, the
youth, impelled by individualistic and democratic ideals
that are incompatible with the authoritarian images and
symbols politically associated with Marxist thought. In
this new *Stimmung,* the dissemination of criticism of totalitarianism and of dissident reports about the gulags
could reach a large public by way of the "new philosophy,"
which had an "overall positive" effect. It was also in this
context that events in Afghanistan and Poland proved
what neither Budapest nor even Prague had fully suc-
ceeded in communicating to French intellectuals: the
true nature of contemporary communism—not the socialist state whose incidental deterioration had to be misrepresented to French working-class communists, but indeed the totalitarian and even imperialist state.

In truth, and this is where Heidegger comes in, people

who have long had more than a few doubts about the democratic nature of the Soviet regime and about communist criticism of the liberal societies did not wait for more favorable times before deconstructing the two faces of the "administered world," in the capitalistic West or in the bureaucratic East. Whether mediated by the work of Hannah Arendt or that of the later Merleau-Ponty, the influence of Heidegger's phenomenology is evident in writers otherwise as disparate as Claude Lefort, Cornélius Castoriadis, and Michel Foucault. We may now be persuaded that criticism of the totalitarian world as the abolition of the primordial division of the social, and of ideology as a forgetting of the "split" (Lefort), is not unconnected with Heidegger's reading of metaphysics as the obliteration of difference and otherness owing to the fantastic plan for total control over a world that has become perfectly transparent and manipulable by the subject. Castoriadis's denunciation of the Soviet system as a "stratocracy" that aims, in a new form of imperialism, at "brute force for the sake of brute force" independent of any reference to an idea whose core was crushed by the ideo-logical machine also calls to mind Heidegger's criticism of the world of technology as the will to will, as the will to increase force for the sake of force outside of any objective or substantial end. How can we conceive of the designation of Cartesian reason as a metaphysical norm from which precisely unreason—the madness of difference and otherness—can't help but be marginalized and then "sequestered" (Foucault), outside of that "history of Being" in which, according to Heidegger, Descartes was the chief author of the forgetfulness of the ontological difference?

The story of Heidegger's charisma and influence in France remains to be written: these influences extend well beyond the circle of orthodox Heideggerians (Beaufret and his students) or even dissidents (Derrida and his students), and here we would have to follow numerous twists and turns to reconstruct a highly complex history.

What is already clear, however, is that the general defection from Marxism has made plainer the presence of thinking that until now followed only in the shadow of its fraternal enemy. We cannot overestimate the amount of political purification that went into the translation of Heidegger's philosophy into a "leftist" intellectual context: his work was thus disencumbered of political connotations that are built into its style and plain to any German reader; furthermore, as a critic of both the totalitarianism of the East and the bureaucratic, repressive, disciplinary, and consumer-oriented society of the West, Heidegger could without demurral personify the weightiest critical authority since the death of Marxism—an elevation that would be unthinkable in Germany, where Heidegger is, and will probably long remain, along with Nietzsche, an accursed thinker.

The taboos and obstacles that could legitimately work against Heidegger were cleared away so well that at the end of this process the leftist intellectual could finally dare to draw directly from the source, thus sparing himself the mediations and "decontamination chambers" that were still de rigueur in the 1970s (Arendt, Merleau-Ponty, Lévinas, to mention only the most important ones). What's more, the profits reaped were substantial: for the intellectual who had given up the totalitarian illusion of a radiant future, and had converted late, grudgingly, to human rights (grudgingly: what indeed could be more banal than this pathetic return to good sense, than this collaborationistic concession to the touchstone of a liberal ideology that one had been so deftly taking to pieces with the help of Althusser and Foucault in the 1960s?), until a few months ago Heideggerianism made it possible to hang onto the essential thing: the crepuscular task of salvaging thought from the general collapse of humanity into American-style businessism.

Against the critics of criticism, against those who attacked Marxism and Heideggerianism as two contempo-

rary strains of antihumanism, and thus "risked" a calcu-
lated reconciliation with the democratic world—in short,
against the thought of the 1980s—it became possible,
thanks to a purified Heidegger, to reinstate the figure of
the critical intellectual and to foist onto the contemporary world a 1960s attitude about the consumer society or
mass culture.[19]

For all its irritating flatness, Farias's book suddenly prevented thinking in circles and struck a discordant note in
the new *consensus* of critical intellectuals. The scenario
is familiar: what is happening to Heidegger is what happened to Marxism in the 1970s. The fact that in both
cases it was in the media that the story unfolded of the
connection uniting the two greatest critical lines of
thought of our time with totalitarian adventures should
not blind us to what is basic: *whether presented in the
name of a radiant future or a traditionalist reaction, total
criticism of the modern world—because it inevitably
leads to seeing the democratic project as the prototype of
ideology or metaphysical illusion—is structurally incapable of fulfilling, except contemptuously and grudgingly, the promises that are also those of modernity.* Why
can't we see that between "collaboration" and external
criticism there is the possibility of internal criticism in
which the positivity of the democratic world can be cen-
sured for the promises it makes without always keeping
them?

The virtue of Farias's book, whatever its weaknesses (to
which we shall return), is to make us rethink a question
that surely would have been once again swept under the
rug by a consensus of intellectuals: under what circumstances can the contemporary world be subjected to criticism that is not inexorably attended by a sweeping negation of the principles of democratic humanism?[20] We need
to spell this out: the neo-Heideggerianism of the 1980s
played a game in which all the moves are familiar. Why
can't we see that the main drift of Heidegger's thinking

was that, from the birth of subjectivity to the world of technology, the sequence is inevitable? Why can't we realize that under these circumstances criticism of the contemporary world is basically—*Heidegger himself knew this and said it plainly*—radically incompatible with the minimum of *subjectivity* needed for *democratic* thinking, in whatever form we conceive it? Mustn't we give the idea of democracy a meaning—if only, once again, a minimal one—and assume not only pluralism (which, if necessary, Heideggerianism could conceive of), but also the possibility for human beings to be somehow the authors of the choices they make, or should make, in common? In short, how can we think of democracy without imputing to man the minimal will and mastery that Heidegger denies him because will and mastery in some sense already contain the seeds of the world of technology conceived of as the "will to will"?

This is the real question. After Marx, Nietzsche, Freud, and Heidegger, it is philosophically impossible to return to the idea that man is the owner and controller of the whole of his actions and ideas. We now know how illusory and dangerous the negation of the unconscious, in all its various forms, can be. This observation should not, however, lead us to adopt a philosophical position that, under the cloak of radical criticism, coolly deconstructs subjectivity when the real task today, *after this criticism and not merely opposing it,* is to rethink the question of the subject.

And on the political level: the anxieties aroused by the democratic universe are legitimate; who could deny it? They are understandable when we identify the true dynamics of this world, which involves the progressive erosion of traditional forms and content and, for that very reason, the springing up of an infinite number of questions. This is the situation we face: in the fields of ethics, law, science, aesthetics, and even religion, the end of traditions and the progress of individualism have made it nearly impossible to consult established certainties with no other form of discussion. It is undeniable that this situation is disquieting and that our subjection to this chronic instability is even tragic: the problem facing the individual in the democratic world is that of limitation and the basis of this limitation. Today we see it most clearly in the bioethical questions about which the very people who ten years ago were militating for the right to abortion are appalled by the prospects for genetic manipulation, the plan of painlessly ending the life of abnormal newborns, or the inextricable legal and emotional conflicts stirred up by surrogate motherhood. Nevertheless, didn't the issue of abortion already involve the same plan of control (over the self, over one's body, over one's destiny), whose present extensions are essentially no different? Faced with this indefinite extension of the individual's control over his own destiny, the whole question (and one could give many examples) is knowing how and by whom the limit is to be set, *whether in the name of a tradition that is still lacking or in a democratic way through public decisions based on public discussion and argumentation by the subjects.* That, for Heidegger, the answer to this question was hardly in doubt should once again inspire us to be prudent in dealing with his criticism of the modern world as the world of technology.

Hence the cognizance we should take of the Heideggerian strategies for "purifying" Heidegger, the intellectual tactics for artificially separating his criticism of democratic modernity from his involvement with the Nazis; for in this game we risk again losing sight of the philosophical and political question raised by modernity.

1

The Heidegger Case

A remark is in order about the trouble necessarily involved in any attempt to deal with the Heidegger case without partiality. One should distinguish between the man and his work, and Proust was surely correct in his quarrel with Sainte-Beuve. The problem, which the exegete cannot deny without compromising the results of his efforts, concerns Heidegger's publication of two kinds of writings of an extreme unevenness: on the one hand, the writings in which Heidegger sets forth his philosophy; on the other hand, the public or private discourse whose very form—speeches, proclamations, reports, letters, and the like—have an indisputably different status from his books, lectures, and courses. Now there are basically two ways, symmetrical and inverse, of delineating the problem posed by this difference:

One can refuse to acknowledge this unevenness, and put *Being and Time* on a par with Heidegger's calls to rally to the cause that found its embodiment in the Führer; this is the course Farias has taken, and it may be that the *interpretative* (not the *documentary*) aspect of his book is much the poorer for it. For we run the risk of simplifying or even missing the most important question: whether the complex articulation between a political involvement and a thinking whose content cannot be claimed a priori to reduce to what was invested in this involvement—except, of course, to lapse into a caricature, the one, for example, that led Pierre Bourdieu a few years ago to reduce, without any other form of trial, the meaning of the ontological difference to the expression of a social will of distinction.[1]

One just as seriously misses the question, however, if, because *Being and Time* is not comparable to a report for a university commission or an address to a student assembly, this difference is changed into one of exteriority. As much as a political reading of Heidegger cannot blot out a disparity between these writings that prohibits reducing some of them to others *without remainder,* so may a certain way of stressing the heterogeneity of the texts and documents to be interpreted lead to a dismissal of the view that they contained material for interpretation: the fact that Heidegger's thinking cannot be *reduced* to what might serve as a link to his allegiance to Nazism does not justify considering only this *remainder* in it, which in its way would also be *reductive.*[2] If this were so, we would find largely blocked the chance (thanks to the current debate) finally to see what cruel limits are soon reached by the attempt to place his thinking, and above all his criticism of modernity, at the service of ideals, those of democracy, to which the very principles of his criticism contain the most absolute of challenges.

Beyond these considerations about method, it must in any case be acknowledged that in confronting the dossier put together by Farias, the French Heideggerians, or the intellectuals administering Heideggerian thought, have produced more or less subtle variations on a single theme: that of evasiveness. Along this line two standard strategies have been cultivated with care and occasional entanglement, even though they plainly contradict each other.

The Dispute about the Facts

In another time and climate of opinion, some people couldn't even conceive that Khrushchev's revelation of

Stalinist terror was anything other than a gross falsehood. Here, the response is repeated ad nauseam: "a shameful falsification," Farias's book has been said to be "inspired by a desire to cover up the truth";[3] "a delirium of interpretation," "calumnious denunciation," the book is said to be a "sham" based on a "weird mixture," consisting wholly of "insinuations" that, "in Heidegger's lifetime . . . would have been libelous";[4] a "procurer" obsessed by the thesis he sets out to prove, Farias "truncates quotations, ignores evidence to the contrary, overlooks the writings in which Heidegger 'explains himself' concerning Nazism, and is not above stooping to a primitive and arbitrary psychoanalysis to flush out the antisemitism in a work that is free of it."[5] In short, the suspect is someone other than we thought: we should methodically "distrust this book"[6] and realize that what we took for a fairly conducted trial was in fact merely a version of the play *"The Affair of the Courier of Lyon* for a slightly higher-browed public"— just barely, moreover, for most of the people who, "as in the play by Alain Decaux and Robert Hossein, pressed on little keys to pronounce 'guilty' or 'not guilty' . . . have never read Heidegger."[7] A short time ago we were urged to terrorize the terrorists; the lesson has been remembered; judge the judge, challenge the jurors, and let us live in peace with the thought.

Beyond what it allows, (namely, avoiding having to really take the facts into account), what should we think of this first obfuscation? Is Farias's case so weak that some people are only pretending to believe it? The book certainly contains some errors and even, we agree, a certain dishonesty. Heidegger's defenders have been unsparing in their efforts to spot inaccuracies or the signs of partisanship: the shortness of the more or less identical lists drawn up is in itself significant.[8] Hugo Ott, the most noted specialist on the question in Germany, has drawn attention to the doubtful points:[9] the erroneous use of a passage from the memoirs of a contemporary to describe

Heidegger's education at Konstanz; a poor understanding of the anti-Semitism imputed to Abraham a Sancta Clara, the seventeenth-century monk whom Heidegger wrote about at the beginning and end of his life; confusion about the location of Sachsenhausen, mentioned by Heidegger in a lecture in 1964 and incorrectly identified by Farias as the concentration camp of the same name.

For all that, does all this call for seeing in Farias's undertaking "a Stalinist trial in its pure form," as the French Heideggerians would at any cost have us believe? [10] Ott's judgment is far more moderate: certainly the Farias book is occasionally lacking in the proper methodical rigor, but he emphasizes, we should also recall how "for decades," "the line of Jean Beaufret, loyally toed by François Fédier," prevailed in France to organize an "apologia for Heidegger" on "method" about which "much could be said"; certainly not everything reported by Farias is new, but "for France," where "Heidegger's political past was misrepresented and minimized to the point of insignificance," the book "is still quite new enough"; certainly, "in matters of interpretation, Farias's book proves problematic," especially with regard to "the relation between Heidegger's political practice and his thinking," but "the virtue of Farias's work consists in the compilation of new sources, and in their positive elaboration." [11] In short, concludes Ott in spite of his reservations, there are in Farias's book "many facts."

The facts, like it or not, are unyielding, and their accumulation impresses even the most skeptical: after solemnly declaring that "this book is deeply unfair" and, weighing his words, calling it "dishonest," Philippe Lacoue-Labarthe recognizes, on the next column of the same paper, that "as for its strictly documentary compilation, Farias's book contains nothing to complain of; the facts cited are to my knowledge indisputable and there are certainly others." [12]

Let us be clear: the point is not to defend Farias's book,

which for us merely plays the role of an extraordinary revelation. What is called for to advance the debate is not the abusive exploitation of the inadequacies and errors in *Heidegger and Nazism* in an endless caviling about established facts. Thus it has become public knowledge that Heidegger loyally paid his dues to the National Socialist party until 1945, that his political activity remained vigorous after his resignation from the rectorate, that in 1935 the minister of education put up his name for the deanship of Freiburg University, that in 1960 he was still in contact, to the point of affably dedicating one of his books to him, with Eugen Fischer, the former director of the Institute of Racial Hygiene in Berlin, and so on. There is, from a simple documentary viewpoint, a whole background to Heidegger's work that can no longer be ignored. And even on the question of anti-Semitism, which can legitimately be debated (since it is also a fact that Heidegger disagreed with Alfred Rosenberg about the biological basis of racism), it is not certain that Farias was as unfair as some would have us believe and that, *even in this area*, one should not be more cautious than Heidegger's defenders. By itself, the loyalty to Eugen Fischer would be a sign of what might have been complicated in Heidegger's attitude and of the need to revise instant judgments.

In 1977, André Glucksmann, who argued that from Fichte to Hegel to Marx to Nietzsche, "all the thinkers in nineteenth-century Germany" were born dressed in anti-Semitism, concluded: "Paradoxically, it was not until Heidegger that a German philosophy appeared that was not anti-Semitic. . . ."[13] Ten years later, this paradox, despite its enormity, has too often been elevated to the point of utter certainty, since people rushed to charge Farias with a maniacal urge to find in Heidegger "an anti-Semitism all the more insidious for never having been expressed,"[14] and said that if there was one feature of Nazism to which "he was resolutely opposed," it was "anti-Semitism."[15] Does Farias situate Heidegger's intellectual education in a traditionalist Christian setting where (notably, through the cult of Abraham a Sancta Clara) anti-Judaism goes without saying? This will be a total loss; both before and after Farias's book, a perusal of Heidegger's political writings of 1933–34 suggests with good reason that "they are overwhelming," but it is emphasized that they contain "no trace of the anti-Semitism that is a decisive component of National Socialism."[16]

We agree; even in 1933–34, Heidegger's speeches and proclamations do not yield any evidence of anti-Semitism, and, as has frequently been stressed, he was opposed to the biologism that Rosenberg saw as the basis for anti-Semitism.[17] For all that, can one impute a "primitive and arbitrary psychoanalysis" to Farias's effort to "flush out anti-Semitism where none exists"? It will probably be said that we should take particular care here to distinguish between the man and his work. We have three remarks, however, on this subject which is so delicate that it perhaps calls for subtler judgment:[18]

Is it really credible that a sensible and responsible person who joined the National Socialist Party in 1933 could do so without at least "concealing" the anti-Semitic "component" and by being so naive or blind as to imagine it "possible to separate the racism from the movement"?[19] Who—above all, what intellectual who is in principle an attentive analyst of ideas and texts—could imagine that racism in the Germany of 1933 was merely one aspect of Nazism, one not consubstantially bound up with it and its constitutive principles? Rather than dreaming up an unlikely compromise with the unacceptable and attacking what is despicable in this compromise, isn't it more plausible to suppose that Heidegger knew what he had to about Nazism and hence could recognize a *certain* anti-Semitism in himself? Certainly he never subscribed to a biological basis for it (nor to the exterminative fate), but in some of its fantasies, anti-Semitism readily linked up with the idea that a lack of rootedness, in whatever sense one understands rootedness, was not exactly a sign of authenticity.

If this is not so, how is it that Heidegger put up with conjugal and professional cohabitation with persons for whom the thematics of race was decidedly not a matter of simple compromise? This is true, first of all, of his wife, and Farias recalls how Elfride Heidegger-Petri, in a 1935 article, called on "the German woman" to realize herself as "the bearer and guardian of the precious racial heritage of our Germanness," and condemned the "fatal error of believing in the equality of all human beings" and of disregarding "the diversity of peoples and races."[20] One is not obliged to share the convictions of one's wife, nor committed to the way she expresses them. Could, however, a *public* figure of Heidegger's status and renown agree to his wife's *publishing* these phrases if he quarreled with the principles that begat them? Similarly, could he cohabit professionally on the list of lecturers of the Deutsche Hochschule für Politik in Berlin,[21] during the winter term of 1933–34, which included characters like Hess, Goebbels, Göring, or Rosenberg, if this collaboration at an institution where his classes came after those of Walter Gross, the director of the party's Department for Racial Purity, made no sense to him? *Credo quia absurdum:* certainly, it may all the more easily be believed that it is most absurd, but, pushed to that point, we must agree, the cult of paradox eludes all rational argument.

If, perchance, one is not persuaded by these two observations, the latter one, which bears on the extraordinary "Baumgarten Report," whose existence seems to have been known, but has rarely been mentioned:[22] in 1933 Heidegger addressed a confidential report to the organization of Nazi professors at Göttingen to warn them about the university's proposal to name Eduard Baumgarten to the chair of professor. Rector Heidegger's report includes the following sentences: "By family background and intellectual orientation Dr. Baumgarten comes from the circle of liberal-democratic intellectuals surrounding Max Weber. During his tenure here, he was anything but a National Socialist." And, for good measure, Heidegger adds that Baumgarten (who was, moreover—the detail is not lacking in piquancy—an old family friend) "was closely linked to the Jew Fränkel," "found protection by this way," and that in the course of his stay in the United States he "became considerably Americanized." Conclusion: "I regard Baumgarten's becoming a member of the teaching staff as improbable as his joining the SA. . . . I have excellent reasons for doubting the sureness of his political instincts and capacities for judgment." Reading this passage from Farias, who moreover presents it evenly and without exploiting everything contained in the document (the text, it is true, speaks for itself), François Fédier has the incredible effrontery to criticize the book for neglecting to point out "that Baumgarten was not Jewish," and that two years before, "Heidegger had turned down Baumgarten's candidacy in favor of that of a Jew"![23] In 1933, what could be more efficacious, when one is talking to Nazis for the purpose of vilifying a Gentile, than to say that he is Jewized and Americanized? Once again, is there anything here indicating that Farias's book is a piece of fakery? Further, did Baumgarten have to be Jewish for the report to be hateful? Is it really necessary to explain that, beyond the evidence here of a bizarre contamination of scholarship by politics in the judgment of a colleague, the reference to "the Jew Fränkel" betrays the hand of a vulgar anti-Semite? Fédier would hardly put up with this kind of talk from any French politician or official without accusing him of racism.

We are forced to conclude that, even in this delicate chapter of the Heidegger dossier, disputing the facts has little impact: the book is no doubt disputable, but where the facts cited are "indisputable"—the possibly unintentional or reckless judgment of Philippe Lacoue-Labarthe is in great danger of being hard to dodge. Thus, a second strategy had to be added to reinforce the initial one, even at the risk of contradicting it.

The Rejection of the New

Faced with the documents Farias had assembled, one is tempted to turn up one's nose: "Clearly, most of the documents put forward by Farias to support his arguments are not as original as one might think and they do not bring conviction."[24] Unless one opts for the blasé style: "For most of these 'facts,' I have not found any in this study that have long not been known to people with a serious interest in Heidegger."[25] The immunization against any novelty likely to upset the established certainties may sometimes even approach the condition of punctureproof armor plate: "All the texts attesting to Heidegger's unyielding opposition to the political and racial furor of Nazism has been known for quite some time now. Any of us can consult the dossier which Heidegger himself summarizes in two texts which have been translated into French."[26] *Sic.* At this rate, with the partisan looking like the only authoritative source, how was it that Farias's book was not seen as an exercise in pure slander in which, by definition, there couldn't be "anything that wounds, nor even touches"[27] Heidegger's thinking. In short, according to a superb witches' brew, everything was known and there wasn't anything there to know. Therefore, one will go on unruffledly managing the inheritance: nothing happened, nothing could have happened, and that is why your daughter can't talk.

Someday it will be necessary to wonder what, in the style of discourse initiated by Heidegger and cultivated with uncommon piety by his disciples in France, could elicit reactions of this kind, testifying to a total inaptitude for calling into question and an unfailing rejection of reality.

For, to say things quickly, the reopening of the dossier of "Heidegger's Nazism" by Farias's book proceeds, merely at the *factual* level,[28] in at least three directions:

1. Neither the readers of the interview that appeared in *Der Spiegel* in 1976 nor the students of Jean Beaufret could ever have suspected the place that Heidegger's political involvement had in his career.[29] Thanks to Farias's investigation on his formative years, at Konstanz and Freiburg, on the start of his university training in 1923 at Marburg, we now know that, well before 1933, a certain ultraconservative and fundamentalist militancy was in no way alien to Heidegger: this is the first legend to come unstuck, that of Heidegger as a total stranger to political matters and invited to take an interest in them in 1933, as though in spite of himself, under the combined pressure of circumstances and colleagues begging him to accept, to the point of martyrdom, the post of the rector of Freiburg University.[30]

2. Reading Farias, we discover also with amazement that Professor Heidegger, during his rectorate and afterward as well, was an extraordinary activist, mounting actions at the bidding of party authorities and conceiving a multitude of plans of the kind to "revolutionize" the German university ever more deeply and radically. A second legend is exploded here: Heidegger was not committed to try to save what might still have been salvageable, but his constant and thought-out goal was to make the university a decisive instrument of the ongoing transformation. "The National Socialist revolution rings in the total collapse of our German existence [*Dasein*]," he proclaimed to the students of Freiburg on 12 November 1933, adding that they were to participate in this overturn through "the creation of the future university of the German spirit," that for which the rules of their existence must not be "principles or 'ideas'": "The Führer himself, and he

alone, is the German reality of today, and of the future, and of its law."[31] We now know that this apologia for the "revolutionary collapse" did not remain a mere pious wish, and we see, correspondingly, the prodigious falsification of the facts to which Heidegger gave himself in his exercises of self-interpretation.[32]

3. As painful as information of this kind can be, it must be agreed that Heidegger did not hesitate to avail himself of any means, up to and including (we have seen this in the example of the "Baumgarten Report") writing letters of denunciation to the Nazi authorities: Heidegger was not an intellectual lost in a domain where the fragments of the pre-Socratics counted less than violence or cowardice and rather belatedly perceiving that his good intentions had been misguided; he acted as a high-level university administrator convinced that the end justifies the means when he considered that loyalty to National Socialism was at least as important as scholarly competence in assessing the qualifications of teachers to occupy a university chair and hence to "actualize the German university of the future."[33]

Confining ourselves to just these facts,[34] we have simply one question: is there truly nothing here "that was not long known to people with a serious interest in Heidegger," nor "anything that wounds, or even touches his thought"? For, finally, if no one knew these facts, why not have them disclosed and thus initiate some genuine thinking about them *in all their seriousness?* And if one may as easily suppose that Heidegger's political involvement in no way contaminated the purity of his philosophical venture—in other words, if one doesn't even consider whether the debate had any substance—isn't it precisely because the duration and intensity of his involvement have been so minimized that the problem won't come up? Let us add, in full knowledge of the case, that if the question of the political involvement of a thinker cannot be fully settled in the arena of his philosophy, we would be paying a highly ambiguous homage to that philosophy by a priori assigning it no responsibility in choices as essential and deep-felt as the ones we are considering here.

The analysis of the reception of Farias's book by the French intelligentsia confirms the hypothesis we advanced in our introduction. So much refined obfuscation, such acrobatics in disputing the self-evident, mask a profound turmoil. To the degree that a very large part of this intelligentsia embraced the major themes of Heidegger's criticism of the modern world, the very idea that this criticism might overlap with Nazism has become intolerable: never, for this reason, has Heidegger had so many defenders in France than in this third debate triggered by his political involvement.

The refusal to acknowledge the synthesis that Farias has contributed to the question thus stems, logically enough, from a defense of threatened intellectual interests. What's more, an interrogation is called for: aren't the extent and seriousness of the facts compiled by Farias of a kind to render ever less credible the most frequently proposed interpretations by Heideggerians of Heidegger's Nazism? Up to now, these interpretations have attempted, with fitful success, to preserve in his writings a kind of "hard core" questioning of humanism and modernity, which was thought to be free of any contamination by Nazism. The reopening of the dossier no longer permits a resort to these tactics.

2

From Humanism to Nazism: Heideggerian Interpretations of Heidegger's Nazism

We shall set aside the zero degree of interpretation, which would be simply to refuse to look at Heidegger's philosophy if not through the lens of his involvement with Nazism, at least in relation to it. How, after Farias's book, could it still be argued, as Jean Beaufret did in 1984, that "Heidegger never did anything to give grounds for the allegations against him," and that the *political* questioning of his philosophy betrays "the conspiracy of mediocre minds in the name of mediocrity"?[1]

A searching examination is in turn called for of one interpretation, long customary among Heideggerians, that relates Heidegger's Nazism to the fact that his ideas in 1933 were not fully disburdened of his earlier "metaphysics of subjectivity" and its consequent humanism. Philippe Lacoue-Labarthe expressed this view in his claim that "Nazism is a humanism." So we need to spell out this interpretation and compare it with the reality of the dossier against Heidegger.

The Orthodox Interpretation

The argument is fairly simple and consists in pitting Heidegger II against Heidegger I: some years ago, certain "orthodox Heideggerians" argued, against Beaufret, that the "rectorate episode" held no material for philosophical interpretation, but they attempted this interpretation from

a strictly Heideggerian position, one that Heidegger gradually constructed by drawing inferences only after 1934
from the "turning point" in the ideas sketched in his 1929
lecture "What is Metaphysics?" One of the authors of the
present book subscribed to this interpretation, and he can
now say in full knowledge of the case how seductive it
was and what intellectual comfort it brought by sparing
him a painful requestioning of the main points.[2] May he
be allowed to add that on reading what the neo-
Heideggerians are saying today, he has the occasional impression that they are discovering America?

At the time, this attempt of the Heideggerians did take
at least a few facts into account, to wit, the extreme "revolutionism" found in the writings of 1933–34: though
Heidegger clung to the project of a "total overturn of the
German Dasein" by the National Socialist revolution, it
was on the basis of a certain idea of decline, one that
prompted him to say in the Rectoral Address that "the
spiritual strength of the West" is failing and to seek in the
Nazi movement under way an alternative to this collapse.
In grasping this idea of decline, however, we cannot but be
struck—this at least was the belief behind the "orthodox
interpretation"—by its apparent prefiguring in *Being and
Time*. This 1927 book announced the central theme of a
critical deconstruction of the modern world as a world of
technology. But how can we speak of decline in the contemporary world without immediately forming some plan
of engagement against this world? And how, under these
conditions, could this engagement not risk looking like
an attempt to return to a "premodern" world? All the ambiguity was there: Heidegger described the decline (or, if
you like: the forgetting of the "life with thought" owing
to the tyranny of the "they" or of "publicness" in whatever sense, superficial or not, in which one cares to understand it) as in principle a possibility for man, a *structure*
of human existence (Dasein), and at the same time it
seemed that, as far as *Being and Time* is concerned, this

possibility was electively actualized in what the later writings were to call the modern era. Two problems were thus presented that called for a careful reading of this basic work: on the one hand, how would this idea of decline lead to some possible activism? And on the other hand, according to what logic was this possible activism then determined to have an antimodern cast?

As a matter of fact, *Being and Time* begins with the charge of a decline, that of the idea of Being: "This question [of the meaning of Being] has today been forgotten," for from its birth in Greece ontology "has deteriorated [*verfällt*] to a tradition,"[3] to the point that Being, which "has at some time been discovered . . . [,] has deteriorated [*verfiel*] to the point of getting covered up again."[4] Hence, a decline of thought, as the later *Introduction to Metaphysics* expressed it, and a decline of Being, are comprised in a backing away from the question of Being. How, in 1927, was Heidegger thinking of this twofold decline? Three key passages can serve as evidence:

In §21, Heidegger insists that "passing over the world and those entities which we proximally encounter is not accidental" but an evident source of the historical deterioration of ontology, "an oversight . . . that is grounded [*selbst gründet*] in a kind of Being which belongs essentially to Dasein itself."[5]

In §27, which concerns the "they," Heidegger spells out what mode of being is at issue by explaining that modern ontology has stopped thinking of the worldhood of the world and is increasingly content to deal, under the name of "world," with various beings within the world, because the Dasein has fallen into the "they" and so attends only to the objects of current absorption: "Because the phenomenon of the world itself gets passed over in this absorption in the world, its place gets taken [*tritt an seine Stelle*] by what is present-at-hand within-the-world, namely, Things. . . . Thus by exhibiting the positive phenomenon of the closest everyday Being-in-the-world, we have made it possible to get an insight into the reason why an ontological interpretation of this state of Being has been missing."[6] In short, it is the falling of Being-in-the-world into the ceaseless absorption in the only available beings that is the basis of the forgetfulness of the phenomenon of the world, a forgetfulness that goes hand in hand with the forgetfulness of Being.[7]

In §43a, which deals with the philosophical problem of the reality of the external world, Heidegger establishes man's fall as the source of the historical decline of thought. He shows how the emergence of the problem of the world's reality presupposes a tacit interpretation of worldhood as presence-at-hand—an interpretation that for him constitutes a genuine "disintegration" (*Zertrüm-merung*) of the "primordial phenomenon of Being-in-the-world." We shall not review here what the exact nature of this disintegration and ontological errancy is for Heidegger: §20 and §21 are devoted to it. What *is* essential is the assertion that "the reason (*Grund*) for this [i.e., for the interpretation whereby thinking forgets its question] lies in Dasein's falling and in the way in which the primary understanding of Being has been diverted to Being as presence-at-hand."[8] The reason for the declining history of ontology (the forgetting of Being) must thus lie in the elective orientation of the fallen Dasein toward what is available for absorption; the relating of the deterioration of thought to the human fallenness could not be more explicit.

To remain scrupulously faithful to the main points in the discussion of the fallenness in *Being and Time*, this relating seemed incomprehensible. *Being and Time* emphasizes the "structural" character, so to speak, of the fallenness; belonging to the very being of Dasein, the fallenness is an "existential" and hence defines the " 'constancy' of Dasein which is closest to us,"[9] a "way of being" of all Dasein "as long as it is what it is,"[10] "an essential ontological structure of Dasein itself."[11] Thus, the fallenness is no "accident" that befalls a human being from the outside, but a *Seinsmodus des Daseins* and even a *Grundart des Seins des Da* ["a basic kind of Being of the 'there' "]: a fundamental mode of Dasein,[12] such that when there is Dasein, there is fallenness, just as there are (these are the two other "existential") existence and facticity. Hence the continual recurrence in *Being and Time* of the locution *je schon* ('always already') to indicate that Dasein is "always already fallen"[13] and the expression *zumeist und zunächst;* it is "proximally and for the most part" that Dasein has fallen.[14] In the logic of this structural approach, the fallenness is not conceived as having appeared one day on a foundation of some primordial authenticity: Dasein is such that its fallenness is already accomplished. Now this is precisely what makes it seem strange and, on this basis alone, incomprehensible for Heidegger to relate the *historical* decline of ontology ("Being was at some time discovered but has deteriorated to the point of getting covered up again") to the *structural* fallenness of Dasein (Dasein is always already fallen): for if it is the fallenness of Dasein that underlies the forgetting of Being, and if, as the first page of *Being and Time* suggests, Greek ontology was not yet completely the victim of this forgetfulness, one must conclude that the Greek Dasein was in some sense less lost in the fallenness than modern Dasein. Therefore the fallenness, which in the passages cited is structural, must also be historical and, so to speak, historically variable.

It may have been tempting for the interpreter to attribute considerable significance to this slippage. For the reader of Heidegger consequently had to suppose that fallenness could come about more or less radically—the predicament, under these conditions, being to see how the variability in Dasein's fallenness squares with the structure of the "always already." Now in *Being and Time*, Heidegger sometimes unhesitatingly goes in this direction: thus he says that the "they" whose dominion is one of the most characteristic features of fallenness has "various possibilities of becoming concrete as something characteristic of Dasein [*seiner daseins-mässigen Konkretion*]. The extent to which its dominion becomes compelling and explicit may change in the course of history."[15] A crucial passage containing an explicit shift from the structural to the historical; if Dasein can have different amounts of fallenness, nothing stands in the way of thinking that the Dasein of the "great age of the Greeks" was "less fallen," as it were, than the modern Dasein. But how can we explain these historical variations in fallenness? On whom or what do they depend? Here again, one has to measure the problematic rearrangements that this slippage necessitated in the idea of the "fallenness of Dasein."

Consistent with the structure of the "always already," fallenness should elude any strictly individual determination: in principle, Dasein's "mode of being" has nothing to do with the attitude of any particular Dasein. Now—and here was another troubling indication of the surprising tension inherent in *Being and Time* and its idea of fallenness—Heidegger somehow refers fallen being to individual determinations: isn't this presupposed by the very idea that fallenness is exorcisable or reversible? In this regard let us recall the role of anxiety described in §40, where the experience of anxious Dasein is described as one in which, because the meaning and importance of beings (the "world" as the world of instrumentality) are rendered null, there emerges the brute presence of Being: "Anxiety . . . takes away from Dasein the possibility of understanding itself, as it falls, in terms of the 'world' and the way things have been publicly interpreted. Anxiety throws Dasein back upon that which it is anxious about— its authentic potentiality-for-Being-in-the-world. . . . As Dasein falls, [anxiety] brings Dasein back. . . ."[16] Even though anxiety is described as an uncommon experience in fallenness, this "feeling of the situation" is assigned a decisive function (shared, in §16, by the experience of the unusable tool): the recovery of what was lost in the fall-enness, i.e., the knowledge of our ownmost being, the attention paid to being in its simple presence. In this, Heidegger elaborates a concept of fallenness that includes a possible reversibility: altogether, with a bit of help from chance (which brings anxiety or shows us a tool that suddenly becomes a stranger), man *may*, if he does not let the chance offered him go by, overcome the twofold cleavage that cuts him off from himself and from what is. In this sense, it *does* depend on man whether his fallenness remains predominant or not. We cannot overemphasize the paramount importance of this possibility in the logic of *Being and Time:* it forms the basis for the legitimacy of the *critique* (giving in to the fallenness, if the fallenness is not a simple structure, may be condemned) and for the possible significance of an *engagement* to dynamize the effort to overcome fallenness—a *critique* and an *engagement* that was theoretically excluded by the idea of the fallenness as a pure structure of human existence.

For all this, the question is whether the *reversibility* of fallenness admitted in *Being and Time* did not directly threaten its *necessity;* if the fall may cease, mightn't it never have happened and been unknown, for example, by Greek Dasein? Better (or worse), why couldn't it disappear in a culture where Dasein would take on its anxiety. Thus one could see how *Being And Time* suggests a basis for the decline of thought (i.e., also of the decline of Being) in the fallen being of man. We thereby also see, however, the theme introduced of *man's essential responsibility for this decline*, in the sense that if the "primordial phenomenon of truth" (viewed as unveiling or uncovering, as the emergence of Being) remains covered, it is because "Dasein's very understanding of Being that proximally and for the most part prevails"—(i.e., the interpretation of the real as availability for use) and which belongs to the characteristics of the fallen Dasein (in the world of absorption, hence of instrumentality, in short: in what is to become the world of technology and culture thought of as industry)—"even today has not been surmounted *explicitly* and *in principle.*" [17] *Thus, the task at hand was this surmounting, and it was up to us to undertake it and to carry it through successfully.* How then can we not be tempted to judge that the reworking of the conditions of fallenness in *Being and Time* led to conclusions that the 1927 book, without formulating them explicitly, obviously called for?

For in assigning a human basis to the declining destiny of thought and in giving man the task of undoing fallenness through a return to his own proper ipseity, didn't *Being and Time* open the way to a certain "activism"? The book's idea of decline ultimately laid to rest a possible twist of destiny over the free decision of Dasein, capable of achieving authenticity provided it "*demands* this authenticity of itself" and makes a resolute commitment to overturn its mode of being for the purpose of gaining its ownmost being.[18] Thus this still anthropo-logical dimension of *Being and Time* (in the sense in which Dasein remains the basis of its destiny) could be interpreted as directly related to the involvement of 1933–34. For what does Heidegger say in his speeches and proclamations? Essentially, that the decisive moment has come for determining whether the future will put the long decline that has been the world's history to an end: "Must we, along with the entire West, founder in decline (*Verfall*)?" [19] a decline that "The Self-Assertion of the German University" describes as "a spiritual decline": "the spiritual strength of the West fails and the joints of the world no longer hold . . . this moribund semblance of a culture caves in. . . ."[20] But in the face of this decline, the stance of the rector of the Freiburg University was to call everyone to a genuine conversion of his being: "It is incumbent on you to stay with this process [*Geschehen*], those of you who always want to press on further, those who are always ready," says the "Call to Students" of 12 November 1933.[21] And what is to be prepared? "A return to roots," said Heidegger a few days later, which "would regain that original need of Dasein to preserve and save its own essence."[22] One might think one were hearing *Being and Time* in the rectorate's texts. *Being and Time* had held out the possibility of reversing the decline if man decides to recover the authenticity of his Dasein; the texts of the rectorate are rife with calls to awakening and action[23] and abundantly develop the theme of the "decision to be made,"[24] for the theme of involvement. Here, as in 1927, the future destiny of the world and of thought depends on the effort of each to achieve authenticity. The lone journey, clearly of unfathomed importance: the conviction emerged that a sociopolitical reorganization could promote this return to ipseity, and the march toward authenticity based on the personal experience of anxiety is then accompanied by the verve induced by a new organization of work, the university, and the economy.

What is discussed here as the "orthodox Heideggerian" interpretation of Heidegger's Nazism could nevertheless come to the following conclusion:

> It is very clear that this belief in the positive action of the "National Socialist revolution" (which "rings in the total collapse of our German existence [*Dasein*]") was possible for Heidegger only on the basis of a conception of decline such that destiny and its change of orientation in a determinate direction are attributable above all to man: the rector's activity in 1933 was but the result of the *philosophical* ambiguity inherent in the 1927 book, and the Germans of 1933 needed to be "resolved to action" only because the Dasein of *Being and Time* needed to be resolute in the face of death. What we call a political mistake is in fact fundamentally a philosophical error—pehaps the ultimate deviation in the history of thought, produced by a certain way of philoso-

phizing in which the man is always and everywhere
the center of reference, a way of philosophizing that
Heidegger was to be the first to shake off. The Heidegger of *Being and Time*, however, is not yet that
philosopher. This way of philosophizing, in which
the "episode" of 1933–34, far from being an episode
in the sense of an isolated sequence and unrelated
to the most important thing in the journey, is the
most dramatic manifestation, this approach in
which the stakes of thinking must be reached along
the lines of an inquiry about man, how can we not
see in it the possibly crepuscular footprint of metaphysics and its modes of meditation along a road
that was nevertheless to lead to a different neighbor-
hood? Heidegger himself was to say: 'One does not
get rid of metaphysics the way one gets rid of an
opinion.' We have just observed this. . . . [25]

Twelve years later, confronted with what we now know,
mainly through Farias, of the "Heidegger dossier," what
thoughts does this interpretation prompt?

First, we agree that Renaut had, if not considerable
nerve, at least one merit: he didn't see in the *political* examination of Heidegger's philosophy merely the elements
of a "conspiracy of mediocre minds in the name of mediocrity." He saw this questioning as within the jurisdiction
of an attentive reading with a care to understand what
Heidegger's undertaking had been.

We also agree that, for all this, the proposed interpretation was quite naive: certainly, it kept the main thing
(Heidegger II), already pitting Heidegger against Heidegger, but at what cost? This orthodox interpretation clearly
saw in Heidegger's Nazism the effect of the *humanistic
deviation in his earlier philosophy:* Heidegger was able to
become a Nazi because he still entrusted the destiny of
the age to man's (the subject's) voluntarist effort to return
to himself (to actualize his essence). To be sure, the later

Heidegger, freer of the metaphysical vestiges of humanism and its accomplices, voluntarism and decisionism,
would have not made this mistake; in any case, and this
was obviously the main point, a reference to Heidegger
capable of pitting Heidegger II (Heidegger's deconstruction of the metaphysics of subjectivity and humanism)
against Heidegger I (the still-humanistic and hence metaphysical idea of authenticity, ipseity, and the like) not only
would escape the logic of this mistake but could even
prove to disclose this logic. No doubt the significance of
the operation (to permit better management of the Heideggerian inheritance by liquidating without rejecting the
question of Heidegger's Nazism) was able to cover over its
weakness, which involves an odd paradox: the very thing
that—originating in *Being and Time* and still allowing for
his allegiance to Nazism, that is, a certain sense of that
"ipseity" distinctive of man which Nazism nullified—
was denounced as the very root of what Heidegger later
called his "greatest blunder."

The naïveté of this interpretation is, however, not unrelated to the caricatural misreading that the group led
by Jean Beaufret made of Heidegger's political involvement—*and that is why we must insist that Farias's book
is so important and revives the interpretive debate on
this score:* for, faced with the revelation that 1933 was not
a blunder for Heidegger but expresses a deep and lasting
sentiment, the "orthodox interpretation," long since
abandoned for other reasons by people who thought about
the true nature of humanism, must present a problem for
those who climbed into the still-warm bed. Who can now
be persuaded that it is because Heidegger was then too
"humanistic" that he wrote disparagingly of the relations
between a colleague and friend of his and the "Jew Fränkel," judged that for the university the revolution involves
an effort to "rethink traditional science from the
strengths and demands of National Socialism," and called
on his students not to "drown" their "hard struggle"in

"Christian and humanistic notions"?[26] Fifteen years ago, the "Stalinist deviation" of Marxism was attributed to the contamination of the worker movement by the "fetishism of man" found "at the base of every bourgeois ideology":[27] in the same era of polymorphic antihumanism, one could be tempted—if one were a prisoner of one of the faces of this antihumanism, *but also because one didn't know the extent of Heidegger's involvement in Nazism*—to interpret it in terms of a "humanistic" or "metaphysical" deviation. But today?

Seeing the structure of this "orthodox interpretation" reappear in various guises in the current debate is not one of the minor paradoxes. For example, what else is Alain Finkielkraut saying when he explains things in these terms:

> I am convinced of the necessity of posing, without evasion, the problem of Heidegger's allegiance to National Socialism. From this perspective, we may have to return to the famous contrast between the inauthentic world of the everyday 'where each is the other, and no one is himself' and the supreme authenticity of freedom for death. Death being our most specific possibility, 'unrelated to the *Dasein* of others,' it is the resolution of freedom for death that takes us out of the daily anonymity and gives birth to ourselves. In this, Heidegger sees *authenticity*, the 'distinguishing feature' of man. . . . It is simply probable that Heidegger saw in the heroico-revolutionary bathos of National Socialism an appeal to German *authenticity*, i.e., the political translation of his philosophy.[28]

Let us set aside the possible difficulty, in an approach centered on the contrast between "life with thought" and the "barbarity" of the media (which Heidegger called the tyranny of the "they" and of "publicness"), of not assuming responsibility for the Heideggerian notion of authentic existence, meaning the distinctive human ability to transcend the world of utility and technology and to wrench free of nature and the everyday in an exercise of freedom. Simply to stay within the context of the debate on the "Heidegger case": subscribing today to the orthodox interpretation seems so difficult that we understand better why it was necessary both to dispute the extent of the revival and to condemn its flimsy scholarship. This was basically the price to be paid for shielding Heidegger's thinking from a deeper investigation of its connection with Nazism rather than the price the orthodox interpretation paid in briskly sacrificing Heidegger I (who still spoke of authenticity) for the sake of saving Heidegger II (who abandoned this vocabulary), or even (*but isn't this a minor variant of the orthodox interpretation?*) by sacrificing the real Heidegger to a possible Heidegger.

Hence the reactions to the reception of Farias's book begin to betray their deep logic: to make it possible, with regard to Heidegger's Nazism, to maintain tested interpretative schemes. The consideration of another style of interpretation disturbed by the shock of the book may, from this point of view, usefully complete this analysis.

The Derridian Interpretation

The Derridian interpretation should be distinguished from the orthodox one,[29] perhaps less because its structure is definitely irreducible to the orthodox one than because its explanation of Heidegger's Nazism, far from resting on a simple management of his thought, sees Heidegger's thinking as rooted in a kind of dissident Heideggerianism.

The thesis upheld by Derrida in *Of Spirit* deserves an examination that is all the more attentive as, in the present controversy, a good number of generally less "dissident" Heideggerians rallied with alacrity to what they took in Derrida to be an unexpected "emergency exit."

That is one of the clearest lessons in the dossier compiled by *le Débat*. Listen, for example, to Pierre Aubenque:

> I think that there is a real break—a break in style, in level, a break in thought—between Heidegger's philosophical work before 1933 and the speeches based on the events of 1933, including the Rectoral Address. Derrida has brilliantly shown this in connection with the novel use of the word *Geist* in the speeches of 1933—in this case a banal term, but one whose positive use by Heidegger is new and paradoxically alarming after the "deconstruction" to which he had started subjecting this idea in his earlier books.[30]

So what does Derrida explain? He begins with an observation. Let us state it. In 1927, §10 of *Being and Time* ticks off the ideas to be avoided in interrogating Dasein so as not to become ensnared in metaphysics and anthropology. Among these obstructive ideas is of course that of the "subject," for "*ontologically*, every idea of a 'subject'—unless refined by a previous ontological determination of its basic character—still posits the *subjectum* (*hypokeimenon*) along with it . . ."[31] At the time, the criticism of the term "subject" thus concerned this term's power to mislead one to interpret existence as "presence at hand," which would be incompatible with the specific determination of human existence as ek-sistence (transcendence): speaking of Dasein as a "subject" is to substantialize it, thus to think of it in the mode of a thing. For the same reason, Heidegger says that we should "avoid" the idea "of the soul, consciousness, mind or spirit, the person," but also of "life" and "man," so long as we have not asked or resolved the question of what is meant by these instances "when they are not reduced to things." Thus, the "analytic of Dasein" will be neither a "psychology" nor a "philosophy of life," nor even a "science of the spirit" (*Geisteswissenschaft*) in the sense in which Wilhelm Dilthey, who nevertheless in other respects has Heidegger's approval, used the expression.[32] For when he happens to use the word "spirit"—despite everything in *Being and Time*, since one definitely has to talk—the word always appears in quotation marks:[33] as long as what Heidegger called "the task of a deconstruction of the history of ontology" is unfinished, the precaution is needed to hold the word at arm's length, as it were, and save thought from the charge of virtual contamination that it contains.

In his 1933 Rectoral Address, Heidegger mentions the spirit without the prophylactic quotation marks, if only to indicate what the spirit is not. For example:

> For "spirit" is neither empty cleverness, nor the
> noncommittal play of wit, nor the endless drift of
> rational distinctions, and especially not universal
> reason; spirit is primordially attuned, knowing reso-
> luteness toward the essence of Being.[34]

And Derrida correctly remarks how, in parallel fashion, the whole Rectoral Address grants a central place to the valorization of the spiritual (*geistig*). Far from being wary of the word, Heidegger now stressed it from the first sentence on: "The assumption of the rectorate is the commitment to the *spiritual* leadership of this institution of higher learning." And, we read, "the leaders [*Führer*] are themselves led—led by that unyielding spiritual mission," and that it is necessary "to will the historical spiritual mission of the German people," or that "the *spiritual world* of a people is . . . the power to preserve, in the deepest way, the people's strengths, which are rooted in soil and blood." The remark would be just as valid, we should add, for the other texts of the rectorate, for example, when in the well-known "call" for the plebiscite of 12 November 1933, which concludes with the injunction to make the Führer alone "the law" of German reality, Heidegger defines the students' task as one of participating "in the

creation of the future university of the German spirit."
The fact, then, is not in doubt: the texts of 1933–34 exalt
the spiritual, and Heidegger's discourse is "traversed,
steeped, illuminated, determined (*bestimmt*) . . . by
spirit."[35]

How does Derrida interpret this lexical switch and its
relation to Heidegger's involvement with the Nazis? The
answer is subtle and consists in ascribing to the rector of
1933 a "tortuous strategy."[36] *In principle*, Heidegger never
gave up his deconstructive approach to the lexicon of the
spirit, but in 1933, to set himself apart from the Nazi biologism and racism which appealed to natural forces and
which—as we have noted—he never accepted, he felt con-
strained to muster a "spiritualized" version of the movement that stressed the valorization of the spirit rather
than the celebration of nature. Hence the disappearance
of the protective quotation marks and the acceptance of a
terminology whose deconstruction he hadn't yet completed. A sort of provisional spiritualist ethics, if you will,
triggered by strictly tactical considerations. However—
and this is the point of Derrida's interpretation—doesn't
this supposedly innocuous loss of quotation marks involve a graver loss, even a falling back into a traditional
anthropology inherited from Christianity and into the
metaphysics of the soul, the subject, or the spirit, from
which the 1927 "analytic of Dasein" was meant to extricate thought? Listen carefully to Derrida's hunch:

> What is the price of this strategy? Why does it fatally
> turn against its 'subject'—if one can use this word,
> as one must, in fact? Because one cannot demarcate
> oneself from biologism, from naturalism, from rac-
> ism in its generic form, one cannot be *opposed* to
> them except by reinscribing spirit in an opposi-
> tional determination, by once again making it a uni-
> laterality of *subjectness*, even if in its voluntarist
> form.[37]

These lines call for detailed commentary, for what they suggest, if we take the trouble to unpack and develop it, raises serious questions. To reject one aspect of Nazism (or what seemed to him just one aspect of Nazism), Heidegger adopted an attitude involving three relations to Nazism:

First, he took the risk of "spiritualizing Nazism"[38] by awarding it "the most reassuring and lofty *spiritual* legitimacy." Here, the relation is one of involuntary contribution, through the awkward adoption of a strategy that escapes the person "who believes he controls it."

In the attempt to "redeem" or "save" Nazism through impressing on it a brand of spirituality, however, Heidegger removes the signs of his involvement: his relation to it thus becomes one of involvement/uninvolvement, pseudoallegiance,[39] or critical allegiance, through the construction of a discourse that "no longer *seems* to belong to the 'ideological' camp calling on its dark forces, forces that are not spiritual but natural, biological, and racial."

However—and here's where the trap snaps shut on Heidegger—in the attempt to disengage himself from biologism through demarcation, Heidegger, despite all and especially *despite himself* (surely this is the main point) sets himself up in a relation of compromise or (the term is Derrida's) "complicity" with Nazism; for in opposing Nazi naturalism merely with the determination of the spirit, he reintroduces a face of "subjectness" that as such (seeing man as a subsistent and not as an ek-sistent) contains the idea of an "essence." Hence the reintroduction of the main theme by which the compromise is tragically manifested: that of a "spiritual fallenness," hence the loss of essence that the peoples of the West are experiencing. In the face of this fallenness, an appeal could be pitched to the one people most able to resist this loss of essence, namely, the German people, a "metaphysical people" par excellence and "the most spiritual" and also "the most exposed to danger," because they are caught between the

East and West, between Russia and America as equivalent faces of the forgetfulness of essence. Therefore, on the German people devolves the " 'great decision' which will engage the destiny of Europe, the deployment of 'new *spiritual* forces from this middle place [between America and Russia].' "[40] It's pointless to insist further: through the determination of spirituality as the subjectness of the subject as opposed to the naturality of nature, Heidegger's demarcating strategy is reversed, through what it led to (and notably the voluntarism implied by the theme of the "great decision"), in the worst of complicities.

This hypothesis may seem appealing and even ingenious. It indicates a logic going from *Being and Time* to the texts of the rectorate, a logic that spares at least some of the book of 1927; from this perspective, *Being and Time* can be criticized only for not completing, or at least not carrying far enough, the supposedly necessary deconstruction of ideas like "spirit" that would have obviated the "tortuous strategy" of 1933. Better: we thus see how in 1933 Heidegger could both be a Nazi and not be one (to avoid the biologizing Nazism of an Alfred Rosenberg). To see the benefits of the proposed interpretation and the reasons why it readily won over so many "orthodox Heideggerians," we should note how it made possible two rescues of Heidegger:

First, a rescue of Heidegger: for if he was a Nazi only because he opposed Nazism with a strategy that precluded a more comprehensive deconstruction of the metaphysics of the subject, Heidegger then rescues Heidegger (and Nazism) by saving himself when he later completed deconstructing the spirit. Derrida shows how in 1953, twenty years after the Rectoral Address, Heidegger's commentary on a poem by Trakl contrasts the adjective *geistig* (the spiritual in the Platonic and hence metaphysical sense of the antinatural or nonnatural) with the *geistlich*, which means another listening to the spiritual, this time in the sense of the sacred. Thought of as *geistlich, Geist* has nothing to do with the metaphysical determination of the spirit; the spirit no longer refers to the sphere of the intellectual or the intelligible but is fire or conflagration, and this idea of the spirit, whatever its ambiguities,[41] escapes metaphysics and its terrible potential implications. Thus we find reestablished a first feature of the "orthodox interpretation" of the episode of the rectorate: the aberration was much more a reflection of the unfinished state of Heidegger's thinking at the time than of the ultimate truth of this thinking and thus here again we can pit Heidegger against Heidegger.

The rescue also concerns, of course, the main points of the Heideggerian legacy, i.e., the criticism of the metaphysics of subjectivity and the attack on humanism. For, unlike the orthodox interpretation, Derrida's does not bluntly maintain, without intermediate steps, that Heidegger was a Nazi because he was still clinging to the metaphysics of the subject and its concomitant humanism: the interpretation is that Heidegger attempted to evade a certain Nazism by appealing to an idea of subjectness as spirituality, forcing him into a steady complicity with "the spirit of the times." Except for a refinement, the second feature of the traditional interpretation thus reappears in all its clarity, and we can easily see the reason for the orthodox Heideggerians' satisfaction: the values of the subject and humanism are inseparable from the still-virtual involvements in what they claim to denounce. Witness the generalization Derrida is pleased to draw from his demonstration:

> The constraint of this program [i.e., the constraint forced on those who adopt the anti-Nazi program expressed by reference to "subjectness"] remains very strong; it reigns over the majority of discourses which, today and for a long time to come, state their opposition to racism, to totalitarianism, to Nazism, to fascism, and the like, and do this in the name

of spirit, even of freedom of (the) spirit, in the name
of an axiomatic—for example, that of democracy
or "human rights"—which, directly or not, comes
back to the metaphysics of *subjectness*. Whatever
place one occupies in it, this program faces all the
pitfalls of the strategy of establishing demarcations.
The only choice is the choice between the terrifying
contaminations that it assigns. Even if all forms of
complicity are not equivalent, they are *irreducible*.[42]

A passage that is decisive and fraught with consequences. With regard to Heidegger's Nazism, it not only
clearly reveals the tenuousness of Derrida's renewal (once
again, the point is to determine a correlation between a
thinking still not free of those vestiges of metaphysics
that would subscribe to the idea of a "distinguishing property of man" or the humanistic valorization of the spirit,
and the most frightful forms of ideology or politics). In addition, however, the exact—and formidable—significance
of this interpretation, in which dissident Heideggerianism links up with the most threadbare of orthodoxies, becomes transparently clear: at every point where thinking
is still animated by a "humanist teleology," thinking is
exposed to "terrifying mechanisms" that threaten it with
the worst "inversions" and perversions.[43] This claim
leads Derrida, in a particularly audacious note, to place
Heidegger's publicly proclaimed commitment to the Nazi
cause on the same level as a "sinister passage" from Husserl's "Philosophy and the Crisis of European Humanity"
(in *The Crisis of European Sciences and Transcendental
Phenomenology*, Husserliana, vol. 6, pp. 318ff. [p.352]
[trans. David Carr (Evanston: Northwestern University
Press, 1970], pp. 269–99 [p. 273]) in which the Indians, the
Eskimos, and the gypsies who are "permanently roaming
all over Europe" are excluded from the " 'spiritual' determination of European humanity."[44] In short, we hear his
warning: the worst is never far from the good humanistic

conscience that Husserl, the unsuspectible, is here supposed to incarnate. If we happened not to see what, or whom, Derrida is alluding to, we can quickly get an idea of it if we see his book called by an interviewer "the somewhat acid manner of answering all (?) those who have recently attacked you in the name of 'conscience,' of 'human rights,' and criticized your deconstruction of 'humanism,' and accused you of . . ."—here Derrida interrupts to spell it out: "Of nihilism, antihumanism . . . We all know the buzzwords."[45]

What Derrida seems unfortunately not to notice is that the tune he has opted to play here is also well-known to him and even turns into the old refrain:

Elisabeth de Fontenay: "Heidegger's inability to extricate himself from the ultimate supports of metaphysics—the possibly lingering humanism of his ontology, no matter how free of anthropology—makes him lack that radical shaking up from the outside" and be mistaken about the essence of Nazism; thus we should "take the risk of thinking, against Heidegger and with him, of a modernity that is constitutionally marked by Nazism" as a modernity that is the "zenith of the reign of the essence of technology, itself a product of a metaphysics that—starting with Descartes and from the correlation he established between the cogito and a physicalistic objectivity that reduces matter to extension—will succeed in dominating the whole of the earth"; only "the uncircumventable deconstruction of humanistic subjectivity" could thus, as Heidegger sometimes said of a possible God, "save us."[46]

Philippe Lacoue-Labarthe: "Only Heidegger can enable us to understand" the truth of Nazism and, more generally, totalitarianism—i.e., the "infinitization or absolutization of the subject that finds its operative effect in the principle of the metaphysics of the moderns"; and if Heidegger himself was implicated in what he had helped to unmask, it is "basically against the background of a kind of 'transcendental illusion' concerning the people and re-

storing a subject (of history)," where the analytic of Dasein and the idea of finitude should have forestalled any
allegiance to the "Nazi myth." For Heidegger—who so
ably deconstructed the onto-theological structure of
metaphysics and its modern face as onto-anthropology in
which man as the subject replaces God—"should have"
recognized in Nazi ideology the "onto-typological" outcome of the same process: in the "Nazi myth" in which
the "Aryan type" as a "pure will (of the self) wishing to be
itself" becomes the "absolute subject," the "ontology of
subjectivity (of the will to will) comes to be fulfilled."
Thus, only fools can "misunderstand" and believe that
Nazism is "an antihumanism": in fact, as we know, "Nazism is a humanism in that it rests on a determination of
humanitas, which is, in its eyes, more powerful, i.e., more
effective, than any other."[47]

What are we to conclude from this consensus? Three
observations, leaving aside the background debate which
was mentioned in our introduction and which will be
taken up in the final chapter, on the correspondence between Nazism and humanism:

1. In the diagnosis of Heidegger's Nazism, and more
generally of the "metaphysical" roots of Nazism, it must
be agreed that their truly important nuances do not significantly distinguish the "dissident" interpretations from
the "orthodox" ones. We find further confirmation, if any
were needed, that the Derridian "dissidence" is merely
apparent or tactical, in that his arguments yield merely a
variant—distinguished perhaps and *certainly better ex-
ploitable*—of the most traditional kind of Heideggerianism. In this regard, the debate about Heidegger is once
again instructive, and no doubt the winning over of the
orthodox Heideggerians symbolically puts an end, also
from this point of view, to a legend by unifying French
Heideggerians on the main points (meaning: when the
main points are at stake).

2. Neither Derrida nor his disciples have come up with

a fresh interpretation of Heidegger's Nazism, compared to what the state of the interpretation could have been more than ten years ago. Certainly the moves made in the interpretations can be different and diverse—how could it be otherwise?—but it remains true that the sense of the interpretation hasn't changed *at all* and can be encapsulated in the claim of a Nazi-humanistic deviation by Heidegger.

3. Thus we understand that in the face of the reopening of the dossier that took place ten years ago and was abruptly revealed by Farias, it was then necessary to dispute the facts and to question whether the interpretation should be changed: if not, how can we return to an interpretive framework that, more than a decade ago, was inseparable from the "blackout" adamantly maintained by Beaufret (and first by Heidegger himself) on the radicalness and real duration of an involvement that was then called, significantly, "the rectorate episode"? This earlier relentlessness has been matched only by the current animosity toward Farias's book: in both instances, the reasons for it are shown by the interpretive stakes. Derrida now tells us that he has long known, from Beaufret, that, for example, Heidegger held onto his party card until 1945, and that he also knew that Beaufret was a revisionist:[48] why didn't he say so, and in particular why didn't he take this into account in his interpretive work, if not to protect its symbolic capital?

Beyond these interpretive stakes, the deepest significance of the debate, for which the Farias book and even the discussion of the Heidegger case are merely the occasion, becomes clear: it hinges on—we can see this clearly in Derrida—the criticism of modernity, and what defines it philosophically, culturally, and no doubt also politically, to wit, the outbreak of subjectivity and the values of humanism. The Heidegger controversy merely stands in the foreground of a controversy that has a quite different impact, involving nothing less than the significance attributed to the logic of modernity: if we argue about it so much today, isn't it because Heidegger's deconstruction of modernity provided a considerable part of the French intelligentsia with the bases and style of its criticism of the modern world? More precisely yet, aren't the reactions all the more spirited because to account for the specific terms and full extent of Heidegger's involvement with the Nazis, we have no choice but to wonder whether this aspect of his critical thinking about modernity wasn't related to the way this thinking attributed to National Socialism "an inner truth and greatness"?

3

Heidegger, Nazism, and Modernity

Because it reduces Nazism to a form of humanism, the traditional interpretation of Heidegger's involvement with the Nazi movement cannot ask the real question in all its complexity. The question, however, cannot be dodged: what could lure Heidegger into Nazism and account for his involvement six years after (and not, unfortunately, before) *Being and Time* and lead him to hold even in the 1950s that, despite the Nazis' outrages and wrongheaded ideas, National Socialism still had "an inner truth and greatness"?[1] In fact, as Maurice Blanchot has rightly suggested, it was less Heidegger that left Nazism than Nazism, by changing, that left Heidegger. And when in private the former rector referred to his involvement in the 1930s, he called it a "great blunder," using an expression one would think more appropriate for a child's carelessly overturning the jam jar.

It seems to us that an understanding of Heidegger's involvement and concomitant assessment of National Socialism first requires an analysis of his criticism of modernity. For this, we need to make clear two of his political judgments, which are inseparable from each other, and to show how deeply rooted they are in the logic of his reading of modern times.

1. The first judgment is well known and was expressed in what are doubtless his most controversial utterances. Concerning the official philosophers of Nazism, Heideg-

ger wrote in 1935: "The works that are being peddled about nowadays as the philosophy of National Socialism . . . have nothing whatever to do with the inner truth and greatness of this movement (namely, the encounter between global technology and modern man). . . ."[2] This sentence has fueled a great debate, primarily about whether the version delivered in 1935 already included the explanatory parenthesis that one can read in the version published in 1952: even though the point is much debated, Heidegger always maintained that the parenthesis appeared in his manuscript for the lecture but that, convinced of "proper understanding of my listeners," he hadn't considered it advisable at the time to utter it.[3]

2. In a 1966 interview for the magazine *Der Spiegel* on his assessment of 1935, Heidegger voiced a second political judgment of great importance to the current debate: "Today it is a decisive question for me whether a political system can be created that generally corresponds to the technological age, and what system this might be. I don't have an answer to this question. I am not convinced that it is democracy."[4] Thus we find a prudent but unmistakable doubting of the competence of *democracy* to respond politically to the needs of modernity.

To see how these two judgments fit into Heidegger's thinking is to see how they are part and parcel of something more basic that they have in common: the interpretation of modernity as the reign of technology.

Modernity and Technology

Even though Heidegger's thinking about the essence of technology gradually became more profound (notably through the determination of the technological relation to the world as *Gestell*, as "enframing"), this theme was sounded early on in his work: his 1937 course on Nietzsche and "the eternal return" already mentions "the technological style of the modern sciences," and the "calculative reason" of technology.[5] And, in 1938, in "The Age of the World Picture," we find all the associated elements of what Heidegger was later to call "the technological interpretation of our age":[6] he describes its "machine technology" as an essential phenomenon of modern times, "the most visible outgrowth of the essence of modern technology, which is identical with the essence of modern metaphysics."[7] And if we were to adopt an archaeological style, we would have to go back to *Being and Time*, in which Heidegger, describing fallenness as the advent of the world of absorption (*besorgte Welt*), says that for fallen Dasein "the wood is a forest of timber, the mountain a quarry of rock, the river is waterpower, the wind is 'wind in the sails' ...": between this presentation of "absorption," in which "the Nature which 'stirs and strives' ... remains hidden ... , the flowers of the hedgerow ... the 'springhead in the dale,'"[8] and the later texts on the "subjugating demand" by which the hydroelectric plant "sets the Rhine to supplying its hydraulic pressure, which then sets the turbines turning,"[9] the displacements are not considerable, even in the imagery. In the "atomic age"[10] as in the civilization of "consumption,"[11] the modern era is *consistently* characterized by humanity's desire to have the totality of beings within reach and to acquire the greatest possible power over this totality through the control of all natural energies, including those of destruction: this will to "make completely providable everything that is and can be,"[12] and this reduction of the real to an "inventory" available for "using up"[13] define the technological relation to the world, "this unrestrained and complete technicalization of man and the world"[14] which makes modern man "the functionary of technology."[15]

These views are well-known, as is the fact that Heidegger never ceased to call for thinking of technology on the basis of its essence, which he thought lay in the completion of modern metaphysics as "the metaphysics of subjectivity." Written between 1936 and 1946, the notes

entitled "Overcoming Metaphysics" explain that, understood on the basis of its essence, the term "technology" is
equivalent to that of "completed metaphysics."[16] For
since Descartes the modern metaphysics of subjectivity
has been an anthropo-logy, the thinking of man as the
foundation, and this according to the two traditional
lines, theoretical and practical, of philosophical investi-
gations. As theoretical anthropo-logy, modern metaphysics amounts to thinking that the real obeys the principles
governing the human mind, for example, (in Leibniz)
transferring the principle of reason (a logical or "subjective" principle) to the real itself and, ontologizing it, sup-
posing that *nihil est sine ratione*. This theoretical
anthropo-logy, which culminates in Hegel's assertion of
the identity of the rational and the real, does not by itself,
however, constitute the bedrock for the domination of
technology as "completed metaphysics."

To see the presence of "completed metaphysics" in the
technological relation to the world, we must consider the
practical aspect of the metaphysics of subjectivity: as
practical anthropo-logy, metaphysics thinks of beings not
only as conforming to the subjective principle of rationality but also as "an object for the will." In the course of the
modern investigation of the essence of subjectivity as
will, beings have indeed increasingly tended to have reality only as an object manipulated by the subject to achieve
its own ends, as a tool or a being that is unvaryingly available to the will. Kant's interpretation of the *I think* as *I
want* and particularly his doctrine of the autonomy of the
will set the stage for a technological interpretation of the
world.[17] For until then, the will had been subordinate to
something other than itself, namely, the ends it was assumed to pursue. In Kant, however, practical reason seeks
nothing other than itself; it wants itself as freedom: in
"Kant's conception of practical reason as pure will," it is
thus the very attainment of the idea of will that is at
stake, "the completion of the being of the will," which

becomes a will unconditioned by anything other than itself, "absolute will," or, since it wants nothing other than
itself, "the will to will."[18]

As an essential link in the process of the technologizing of the real, "the autonomy of the will," as Kant understood it, could in fact be separated from the ultimate ab-
solutizing of the will only by a still-indispensable
mediation: that of the Nietzschean theory of the will to
power as "the second to the last stage" of the process.[19]
With the Nietzschean will to power, an image of the will
looms forth that seems to want something other than itself (power), but—according to an interpretation found in
Heidegger's lectures on Nietzsche starting in 1936—it actually wants more power (more domination) merely the
better to test itself indefinitely as the will mastering the
real: in short, "the being of the will to power can only be
understood in terms of the will to will,"[20] on the basis of
this unconditioned will through which the Cartesian project of the ownership and control of nature would be real-
ized. We thus see how Heidegger could judge that in the
reign of technology, "the development of the uncondi-
tional dominance of metaphysics" actually begins by
finding an era worthy of it.[21] For, from Descartes to
Nietzsche, the evolution of reason has consisted—and
here Heidegger's analysis is similar to those of Max Weber
and Max Horkheimer—not in setting goals by itself but
in transforming itself from objective reason, which it once
endeavored to be, into purely instrumental reason.[22] In
parallel, the will is no longer assigned any end: the aim of
mastering the world is not, as in Descartes or in the Enlightenment, to emancipate men and to secure their happiness, but becomes a search for mastery for the sake of
mastery, or, if you will, for "brute force for the sake of
brute force."

We need to keep these claims in mind when we consider the complex question of how Heidegger could see in
National Socialism a movement capable of "correspond-

ing" to this technological development of completed metaphysics.

Two Views of Nazism

The real problem, which is common to the assessment of Nazism's capacity for "corresponding" to the demands of global technology and to the correlative downgrading of democracy as a "political system" incapable of "corresponding to the technological age," lies—how can we not see it?—in the inherent ambiguity in the term "correspond": "correspond" may mean *be in step with* what is corresponded to, expressing it in some way and hence being equal to it and accompanying it; but "corresponding" is also *responding* to what is corresponded to; in this sense, responding to a situation can mean producing a response that is a remedy or solution, or at any rate that *can* provide a solution to the problems posed. Thus we need to consider two interpretations of Heidegger's assessment of Nazism (and hence also of democracy):

According to the first view, in which the correspondence to technology simply calls for a political expression or translation of its requirements, National Socialism had the fundamental greatness of recognizing these requirements and inferring from them the irremediable unfitness of democracy to adapt to what the completion of modernity calls for. Democracy, as a political model based on the idea of autonomy or self-institution, indeed belongs to the register of modernity, but democracy is to National Socialism what Kant's philosophy of the autonomy of the will is to Nietzsche's doctrine of the will to power: a preparatory phase that becomes obsolete upon the debut of what it had been preparing for. According to this logic, democracy is surpassed in the pursuit of a political system better equipped to meet the demands of modernity: like democracy, political modernity surpasses itself in the direction of what it needs, and therefore Nazism represents a sort of political postmodernity that radicalizes what had in its own way already been expressed by democratic modernity.

A second and quite different view also takes as its starting point the same "technological" interpretation of the modern world, in which the ability to "correspond" to the technological age means the *capacity to respond to it effectively by forestalling its dangers.* Here democracy is not impugned for its sluggishness in meeting the demands of modernity but by reason of its enrollment in this same modernity whose essence is expressed today in global technology: how could democracy—as a "political system" that, with autonomy as a supreme value, is one moment of the modern development of subjectivity as will—bring about a response to the problems posed by a globalization of technology that fits into the same logic?

Because of this fact, we know what tremendous difficulties (and inevitable vexations) contemporary neo-Heideggerianism of the left is exposed to when it tries to press Heidegger into the service of a thinking of democracy that tries to conceive of the nation as a "plebiscite every day,"[23] as a constantly renewed adherence to the principles of the social contract: through both its implied valorization of the will and the democratic ideal of the social contract, this congenial idea of the national community is unlikely to find in Heidegger the philosophy it deserves. Like it or not, Heidegger disqualifies democracy as being incapable of responding to the challenge of modernity. *To the contrary,* if the truth of National Socialism lies in its ability to bring about this response, then Nazism is seen not as a postmodern and postdemocratic political system but as an antimodern and antidemocratic movement that will reveal the antidote to the technological logic of modernity that this logic seeks to destroy.

Between these two possible views, how should we understand the appropriate tone for Heidegger's assessment of Nazism and democracy? Here it may be paradoxically less a matter of entirely eliminating one reading in favor of the other than of seeing a real tension produced in Heidegger's work by the inherent ambiguity in his idea of a possible correspondence between National Socialism and the technological age. For all that, beyond the particular case of "Heidegger's Nazism," this tension is not unrelated to the structure of National Socialism in general.

On Nazism as the Achievement of Modernity

The first view, that of Nazism as the political system best "in step" with the globalization of technology, seems to involve two elements in Heidegger's writings.

Some of the writings, from the period of the rectorate and shortly afterward, suggest a conception of the National Socialist revolution as an attempt to go further in the direction of modernity (and technology) than the old democracies were able to. When in the Rectoral Address Heidegger stigmatizes the idea of freedom that, when understood within the university as "academic freedom," confuses true freedom with the simple "freedom from concern, with arbitrariness of intentions and inclinations," he contrasts it with what he calls "the highest freedom," "to give the law to oneself"; better, he stresses that in the act of "self-assertion" as "authentic autonomy," whether by the university or by the people, "we . . . will ourselves";[24] much more than counteracting the modern development of the will in auto-nomy and in the will to will, the question here seems to be one of fitting into the very core of this development and seeing what is left behind, "the road from which one does not return,"[25] i.e., that culture whose "dead appearance" is breaking up and making the edifice of the West totter.[26]

This receives further confirmation in a passage from a 1940 lecture on Nietzsche in which Heidegger lays the blame for the fall of France on the fact the French people was not "equal to the metaphysics born of its own history"—meaning equal to what Descartes had seen when, with the cogitative outbreak of subjectivity, he "broke down the door" to "the sovereignty of the earth"; and the lecture goes on to interpret Germany's victory in a way that couldn't be more meaningful:

> What Nietzsche by that time had already recognized is now apparent to us: that the modern "mechanical economy," the mechanical calculation of all action and all planning in its absolute form, requires a new humanity, one that surpasses what man has been thus far. It is not enough to possess tanks, airplanes, and radio; nor is it enough to have individuals available who are capable of manipulating engines and instruments of this kind; it is not even enough that man should be able to master technology as if it were something inherently neutral, beyond profit and loss, gains and damages, construction and destruction—something usable at anyone's whim for any purpose. For that, a humanity is needed that will be thoroughly conformable to the basic and singular essence of modern technology and to its metaphysical truth, that is, a humanity that will allow itself to be totally dominated by the essence of technology precisely in order to control and make use of the various processes and possibilities of technology.[27]

In this extraordinary passage we clearly see the prospect of humanity's renewal through the integration of the unprecedented needs of modern technology. In the framework of his metaphysics, the next lines spell out Nietzsche's idea that only the "Overman," he who assumes "active nihilism," could "correspond to the absolute mechanical economy": Heidegger's treatment emphasizes the even more imperious need to get beyond "active nihilism" in the direction of a new questioning of Being that would permit a better apprehension of the essence of technology and hence a deeper correspondence to it. It remains no less true that Nietzsche had in his way already "metaphysically" perceived what in our time determines success or failure: the capacity to respond to the call of technology. France's defeat and Germany's victory represent, so to speak, concrete examples of what separates democracy from another political system less deaf to this call.

The same view of the Nazi system's political expression of the demands of modernity that is technologically completing itself comes in other of his writings, though in an admittedly less direct form. This appears in some texts in which Heidegger sketches a reading of the phenomenon of totalitarianism in which he describes it in all its generality as one manifestation among others of the reign of technology. Thus, for example, the passage from the speech "What are Poets For?" thought to date from 1946: "Modern science and the total state, as necessary consequences of the nature of technology, are also its attendants."[28] This goes, no doubt, for a science that has become "an entrapping and securing and refining of the real,"[29] of which we can see how Heidegger finds in it the "enframing" of nature (the *Gestell*) as the process by which technological man "at every turn ascertains a region of the real as a domain of his objects." But totalitarianism? The most thorough explanation is provided in the notes for the years 1936 to 1946, "Overcoming Metaphysics": to ensure the full reign of man over beings, "men must be organized and equipped who serve leadership," men "who are the decisive suppliers and who oversee all the sectors of the consumption of beings"; this guarantee requires that these "leaders" (*Führer*) have a view of the "totality of beings, sectors of consumption" without which the indefinite exploitation of beings would soon reduce to scarcity.[30] As preconditions of an efficacious calculation of consumption, planning and "totalitarianism" are thus part of the essentially technological profile of modernity; the domination of technology brings about the political reign of total domination.

Thus Heidegger, inventing a topos reproduced a thousand times by his disciples, thought he needed to ridicule "the moral outrage of those who don't yet know what is": outrage in the name of values, as for example the values of legal humanism against the instituting of totalitarian systems that represents a blindness to the true "foundation" of this "phenomenon." Authentic meditation on the phenomenon starting from the essence of technology (and, more deeply, starting from the essence of modernity) should, on the contrary, free one as much from outrage as from enthusiasm by unmasking what is "fated" in the phenomenon. In another way, writings of this kind permit Heidegger to see in National Socialism—though we don't quite see how what applies here to the total domination of the führers in general would not apply to it—the political system that best corresponds to the technological completion of modernity: when we add that Heidegger in no way considered the reign of technology a contingent aspect of history but regarded Being itself as being the "essence of technology,"[31] in other words, that he inscribed the advent of technology in the destiny of Being, it is thus a "political system" based on the *Führerprinzip* that is fitted into the destiny where it achieves better than democracy what is required by "completed metaphysics."

On Nazism as a Response to Modernity

In addition to the view of an internal correspondence between Nazism and modernity, Heidegger's thought includes a second view of the relation between them, one that produces a tension with the former view and may be one of the keys to the complex relation between Heidegger's thought and National Socialism. For, parallel to the reading analyzed, Heidegger always saw in the Nazi en-

deavor the search for a third term irreducible to either
Western democracies or Soviet collectivism. His 1935 *Introduction to Metaphysics*, which describes the globalization of technology as the "spiritual decline of the
earth," conjures up the pincers of East-West conflicts in
which Europe is caught: "From a metaphysical point of
view, Russia and America are the same; the same dreary
technological frenzy, the same unrestricted organization
of the average man."[32] A disconcerting passage when read
together with the view expressed in the earlier passages,[33]
for this time Heidegger manifestly sees adequacy of response to global technology as a sign of decadence and
seems to appeal to a third term, which is neither democracy nor collectivist totalitarianism, to counter this decadence: he of course sees this third term in National Socialism, whose "greatness" and "inner truth" would lie in
a relation to technology different from, for example, the
one described in his lecture on Nietzsche concerning Germany's defeat of France in 1940. Against the various political systems in both the East and the West that merely
express the unleashing of technology, Nazi Germany thus
offers a solution, and this is expressed in a lecture on Heraclitus in the summer of 1943: "The planet is in flames,
the essence of man is out of joint. World-historical thinking can come only from the Germans—if, that is, they
find and preserve 'the German essence' (*das Deutsche*)."[34]

What is the logic of this second and *seemingly* quite
different view of the significance of National Socialism?
Here Heidegger points up the idea that the existing political systems of liberal democracy in the West and collectivism in the East constitute merely the two political
forms taken by the domination of subjectivity: "Only because and insofar as man actually and essentially has become subject is it necessary for him, as a consequence, to
confront the explicit question: Is it as an 'I' confined to its
own preferences and freed into its own arbitrary choosing,

or as the 'we' of society?" Thus, in short, both the individual in a liberal society as well as the power and rights of the collective that oppose him in the East are figures of subjectivity, and as such they belong to the modern age: "Only where man is essentially already subject does there exist the possibility of his slipping into the aberration of subjectivism in the sense of individualism. But also, only where man *remains* subject does the positive struggle against individualism and for the community as the sphere of those goals that govern all achievement and usefulness have any meaning."[35]

We are thus obliged to note that, though in this second view (*which does not follow the first chronologically but remains in constant tension with it*) the issue is one of "corresponding" politically to the demands of technology and hence of completed metaphysics, the purpose cannot be to fulfill these demands: that is being carried out in the East as well as the West, "Americanism" and the "Communist movement" being equally, Heidegger was to say in 1966, "determined by planetary technicity";[36] rather, the point here is less to see "the situation of man in the world of planetary technicity as an inextricable, inescapable destiny" than to "help man as such achieve a satisfactory relation to the essence of technicity"; *and, declared Heidegger in 1966, "National Socialism did indeed go in that direction."*[37] Certainly, Heidegger immediately made it clear that "those people, however, were far too poorly equipped for thought to arrive at a really explicit relation to what is happening today and has been under way for the past three hundred years," but it remains no less true that, considered in its "truth," the Nazi movement was on the right track: that of fashioning a "free relation to the technological world," a relation capable of counteracting "Americanism," i.e., the flooding of the products of technology all over the earth, which has turned into "a world market," in which, Heidegger says, what threatens us is of course less the "American" as such than how the "American flood" expresses "the unexperienced nature of technology."[38]

If even in 1966 Nazism appeared as the movement that, unlike democracy, had been headed toward a suitable response to the challenge of technology, it is decidedly difficult, beyond the facts reported by Farias, to cling to the thesis of a momentary involvement or a temporary aberration of a Heidegger to whom "National Socialism *momentarily* appeared the only fitting answer."[39] It would be hard to be more seriously mistaken about Heidegger's relation to Nazism: the real problem is probably not that, as Finkielkraut and many others believe, "knowing he was entirely mistaken, he did not make honorable amends," but that, although he admitted his errancy, his "big blunder" was not his allegiance (in no way provisional, we note) to the principles of National Socialism, but only in his siding with men incapable of living up to them.[40] *Contrasting the true spirit of the movement and Hitler's "deviationism," Heidegger in 1966 did not in any way question the possibility of a "good" National Socialism when he declared that it was in principle impossible for democracy to respond satisfactorily to the problems posed by the infinite domination and devastation of the earth.* Even though in answering the question of what political system can meet the challenge of technology, Heidegger conceded that he did not have an "answer" and suggested that "we have not yet found a path that corresponds to the age of technology," why did he maintain this exception in favor of Nazism? To understand Heidegger's gesture, we need to consider two points:

Democracy is condemned *for being modern and for the same reason as all modern responses to the challenge of technology:* in 1966 Heidegger saw fit to use the term "half-measures" in regard to democracy or the "state based on rights," "because I do not see in them any actual confrontation with the world of technicity, inasmuch as behind them all, according to my view, stands the conception that technicity in its essence is something that man holds within his own hands."[41] In other words, as a modern "political system" based on the values of autonomy, democracy shares in the plan of mastery that defines modernity and makes technology the completion of the modern metaphysics of subjectivity. Under these circumstances, how could it respond satisfactorily to the problems posed by the globalization of technology, particularly the way in which "technology increasingly dislodges man and uproots him from the earth,"[42] and through the flood of "Americanized" products, forces all mankind to enter into "monotonous uniformity in order to keep up with what is real"?[43] Unless we wish to foster incoherence, we have to agree that under these circumstances the typical attempt by "the Heideggerians of the left" to reconcile Heidegger's criticism of technology with democratic values makes very little sense—which does not conversely mean (we will come back to this) that an allegiance to the values of democracy implies a relinquishment of any critical reading of modernity, notably a criticism of instrumental reason.

Like democracy, National Socialism also appeared to Heidegger to involve an allegiance to the development of technology, but National Socialism was different in that it included the principle of an *antimodern* reaction to the perverse effects of this development. Does technological modernity constitute a formidable power for uprooting and uniformitization? "Everything essential and of great magnitude has arisen only out of the fact that man has a home and was rooted in a tradition."[44] And if we still have no adequate answer to "the global hegemony of the unthought being of technology," "who of us would be in a position to decide whether or not one day in Russia and in China very old traditions of 'thought' may awaken that will help make possible for man a free relationship to the technical world"?[45] Against the modern uniformitizing uprooting, there is the antimodern call to *tradition:* here is a decisive element for appreciating the "greatness" Heidegger saw in Nazism, so true is it that he thought he saw in it the capacity—faced with "the forsakenness of modern man in the midst of what is," and ceaselessly given over to its mastery and consumption[46]—for giving birth to a "new unity of rootedness on the basis of which the people commits itself, in its state, to act for its destiny."[47]

We readily see how these strongly held convictions could in 1933 have led Heidegger (in the Baumgarten report) to judge incapable of National Socialist loyalty a colleague both "Americanized" and Jewized, and hence, to Heidegger, doubly cut off from the values of rootedness and tradition. Recreating hierarchies (through the application of the *Führerprinzip*) on all fronts, bringing forth for the German people a "spiritual world" understood as "the power that most deeply preserves the people's strengths, which are tied to earth and blood,"[48] Heidegger saw the National Socialist revolution as linking up to the headwaters upstream of modernity, with the greatness of the Greek beginning in which—the Rectoral Address makes this link to the Greek past explicit—science was not yet "'a cultural good,' but the innermost determining center of all that binds human beings (Dasein) to people and State."[49] Certainly, we can see from his 1942 lectures on Hölderlin, there should be no question of Heidegger's endorsing Nazi ideologists who, determined at any cost to uncover links between ancient Greece and the New Germany, manipulated texts to the point of "having one believe that the Greeks would already all have been National Socialists."[50] Nevertheless, the relatedness of the greatness of Greece to the ongoing movement was not so repellent as not to be affirmed sometimes to the point of caricature in the statements of Heidegger himself, for example, when in the summer lectures of 1933 on "the fundamental question of philosophy"—after interpreting the "primordial Greek thought" recorded in fragment 53 of Heraclitus on war as "father of all beings"—he calmly concludes: "To understand these fragments truly, a different consciousness of the existence of man and of a people is required from what we had until just last year."[51] *Sic!*

Heidegger the Neoconservative

Thus Heidegger developed a less than perfectly univocal interpretation of Nazism, divided as he was between the temptation to see the National Socialist revolution as, on the one hand, a postmodern actualization of modernity, and on the other, the antimodern activity of a humanity linking up, against the decline of Europe, with the great Greek past. This equivocality in his thinking persisted long after the collapse of Nazism: as we have seen in his 1966 interview with *Der Spiegel*, he primarily affirmed the second view, according to which Nazism (at least as it should have been) responded to the challenge of technology; but in 1949, Heidegger wrote the only sentence in which he expressed a view about the Holocaust: "Agriculture is now a motorized food industry—in essence the same as the manufacture of corpses in the gas chambers and extermination camps, the same as the blockading and starving of nations, the same as the manufacture of hydrogen bombs." Certainly, this is Nazism as it was (and not as Heidegger dreamed of it), and despite its shocking but inevitable inadequacy, the analysis here becomes critical: Nazism is restored to the logic of modern technology to which, far from responding satisfactorily, it corresponds to the point of being the direst of tragedies.[52]

How can we explain this tension, and what does it mean? Internal to Heidegger's work, it probably reflects an ambiguity inherent in Nazism itself. In *On Totalitarianism*, which repeats the classification devised by Hannah Arendt, Raymond Aron devotes some pages to a typology of the various types of twentieth-century governments born of a revolution against the principles of de-

mocracy understood as "constitutional-pluralistic regimes": Hitler's, Mussolini's, Stalin's, Franco's, and
Antonio Salazar's in Portugal. In a now-classic analysis of
the common parameters and distinctive criteria of these
regimes, Aron concludes that the Nazi regime was incon-
testably the oddest and most heterogeneous of the lot:
ideologically, through its hostility to modern rationalism
and the democratic principles of 1789, it belongs to the
"authoritarian-conservative" regimes of the Salazarist
type, but unlike Salazar's or even Mussolini's system—
which "was not revolutionary compared to the German
regime"—National Socialism, which was "revolutionary
in the strict sense of the term," "strove to overturn the
social and ideological structures of the Weimar republic."
As revolutionary as the Stalinist regime, but with an ideology as hostile to modern political reason as the authoritarian-conservative regimes, National Socialism, a pure
representative of what is commonly called fascism, had
the additional feature (which also distinguishes it from
the Portuguese and Spanish regimes) of not being established "on the fringe of industrially developed civilization"; in this respect it was modern, for it took account of
the resources of "industrial civilization" and hence represented a peculiar blend of tradition and novelty, antimodernism and modernity.[53] This diagnosis, though in different terms, is shared by Louis Dumont, who also sees in
Nazism a weird blend of traditionalism and hypermodern-
ism.[54]

The tension involved in Heidegger's assessment of National Socialism expresses the same mixture: in the age of
the globalization of technology, conservatism cannot just
pigeonhole the existence of a technicalized world and
withdraw into premodern social or cultural forms; in a
sense, the mission is to implement the technological destiny of modernity, but also actively to counteract it with
the very thing this destiny denies, to wit, the values of
tradition, by attempting to impose these values on moder-

nity by force. The very idea of a "conservative revolution," which defines the specific nature of the National Socialist revolution, thus involves a tension oddly close to the one we find throughout Heidegger's writings.

If we wanted to spell out this linkage further, we should no doubt indicate what distinguishes Heidegger's attitude from the most recent version of conservatism and call its tenets "neoconservative." For the neoconservative mind's characteristic feature is expressed in the tension exhibited in Heidegger's postmodern-antimodern assessment of Nazism: it is necessary to link up with tradition through criticism of what exists (technology) and thus to fight the will with the will. It would of course be absurd to claim that, by itself, this attitude entails Nazism. In the Germany of 1933, however, how could such an attitude not go along with and be sorely tempted to embrace the Nazi idea of a conservative revolution? For all that, to portray Heidegger's neoconservatism as a mere "reflection" of what was then taking place sociohistorically would be to propose a caricature of reductive sociologism: things are far more tricky, and Heidegger took up Nazism for reasons that were *philosophical* and internal to his criticism of modernity.

The Philosophical Ambiguity:
Is Modernity a Destiny?

In its closeness to Nazism, the neoconservative position appears hardly coherent because of its jumble of conservatism and revolutionism, tradition and novelty, antimodernism and postmodernism. Heidegger's neoconservatism, however, stemmed from an ambiguity, even a contradiction, in the deepest part of his philosophy, particularly his "technological" interpretation of modernity. From his thinking we can infer two gestures with regard to modernity:

We know that, for Heidegger, the advent of the reign of

technology is not the product of some human aberration but has its roots in what is at the root of all history, namely, the forgetfulness of Being. This forgetfulness does not have the status of an inattention that is "anthropological" in origin, but must be thought of as "a withdrawal of Being": Being itself—as the difference between the coming forth of beings and their presence as being-present available to human sight or absorption—is that share of invisibility inscribed at the heart of everything visible, or, to quote a formula from "The Anaximander Fragment": "As it reveals itself in beings, Being withdraws."[55] In this sense, *Being is its own forgetfulness* and it is thus Being itself, *as forgetfulness* and hence withdrawal, that leaves man at grips with the mere presence of beings offered for his manipulation: thus, both metaphysics (the forgetting of Being in favor of beings reduced to being an object for a subject) and technology (the infinite machinization of beings for the purpose of consumption) can be thought of as a withdrawal of Being, or of Being as withdrawal—better: metaphysics and technology are basically Being itself, as the just-quoted formula clearly says of technology: "Technology is in essence Being itself."

According to this interpretation of all history as the history of (the forgetfulness of) Being and of Being itself as the history (of this forgetfulness), i.e., as a withdrawal, it will surely be agreed that there would be no sense in rebelling against the reign of technology and trying to thwart it. Even in his *Der Spiegel* interview, Heidegger still asserts that technology is not something man can control: only a change in the times, the emergence of a new "epoch of Being" (in other words, of a new modality of its withdrawal), could produce true liberation vis-à-vis the reign of global technology. Hence the fact that, in the face of this reign, Heidegger could invoke an attitude he called *Gelassenheit* ("releasement"), an attitude consisting less in deploring or combating the reign of technology than in allowing it to deploy itself—and in fact, how could it be otherwise, when technology is nothing other than Being itself? Rather than opposing the unleashing of globalized technology and, for example, combating it with political or legal forms (those of democracy or the state based on rights) that do not correspond to its needs, it is advisable to open ourselves more precisely to what exists and go along with its unfolding:[56] hence the pursuit of a "political system" capable of corresponding to and thus being adequate to the needs of the age of technology may be found to be on course with an interpretation of technology as being essentially none other than Being itself.

At first it is hard to see how this disconcerting plan of action can introduce a parallel will for opposing technology with an effective countervailing response: if technology is Being, why attempt to counteract the unrootedness and technological uniformitization of the world through a reaffirmation of the values of tradition and the soil? In other words, how can *Gelassenheit* be squared with this return to the ultravoluntarist aspect of a reaction against modernity? To pinpoint the solution to this characteristically double-edged problem, which is the key to Heidegger's Nazism, we must briefly reconsider what surely constitutes the central difficulty in this idea.[57]

Although at the level of the forgetfulness of Being (which culminates in the technological completion of modernity) Heidegger rules out the interpretation of this forgetting (and thus of the decline that accompanies it) as a *defect imputable to a subject*, he suggests in the introduction to *What is Metaphysics?* that the "obstacle" preventing man from fully realizing his essence—i.e., from becoming the "shepherd of Being," to use a formula from his "Letter on Humanism"—is the way in which beings (equivalent to the forgetfulness of Being) are thought of by metaphysics.

Here we begin to see the crux of the problem: how can we think of the forgetfulness of Being as an "obstacle" if

Being is its own forgetfulness? Inscribed in Being as it is, the forgetfulness seems external to Being, as though forgetfulness, understood as an obstacle, was to be overcome: if this were so, a basic subjectivity of our destiny could be reintroduced, and with it—far from having "merely to wait" with an attitude of *Gelassenheit*—there could emerge a will to use the conditions of remembrance to oppose the technological radicalization of the forgetfulness; the issue would no longer be just to achieve modernity but also to destroy anything in it that stands in the way of thought as the "memory of Being": antimodernism then becomes an indispensable component of the endeavor.

To understand this displacement, however, we still need to spell out what "obstacle" we are dealing with. If metaphysics is an obstacle to the attentiveness to Being, it is as ontology that metaphysics *seems* to ask the question of Being: "It means all beings as a whole although it speaks of Being. It refers to Being and it means beings as beings." [58] With the result that, owing to the confusion between Being and the being of beings, the forgetfulness of Being goes unnoticed: "Forgetfulness settles into forgetfulness," [59] Being's abandonment of man "remains veiled." The result is the *forgetfulness of forgetfulness*, which doubles and radicalizes the forgetfulness of Being, for thinking of Being is to think of its forgetfulness as a withdrawal (difference)—which presumes that forgetfulness is at least noticed and debatable. The History of Being is thus that of a twofold forgetfulness, a forgetfulness that is doubled through its own forgetfulness. But—*and the whole ambiguity of Heidegger's thinking is here*—the forgetfulness of forgetfulness, strangely, seems referred to man, who is credited with the capacity, and hence also the power of decision, to overcome it: it is important, writes Heidegger, "first to put thought back in the presence of the forgetfulness of Being," but "it remains to be shown whether thinking will be capable of it": here everything depends on our "attempt to learn to develop a regard for the forgetfulness of Being."[60] Thus, when we think of forgetfulness as destiny (as *historial*) and not as a defect, then neither the forgetfulness of forgetfulness nor the remembrance of forgetfulness are thought of as historical: it depends on man, and perhaps also on the human community, whether he gives in to it or overcomes it, thus confronting forgetfulness once again.

This ambiguity has a profound impact on the analysis of technology and modernity:

From what, in the technological completion of modernity, testifies to the forgetfulness of Being, "only a God could save us," declares Heidegger to *Der Spiegel*:[61] global technology and its unleashing can find remission only through "a change in the times." At *best* (but what does that mean?) the task of the "political system" is to bring about what the development of technology demands, if only at the cost of sacrificing the things that modernity has until now exemplified politically, namely, the values of democracy. That is, in relation to democratic modernity: Nazism as postmodernity.

Besides testifying to the forgetfulness of Being, however, the unleashing of technology helps to cover over this forgetfulness by creating the conditions, through the illusion of a total absence of distress, for the greatest of distresses, the one in which humanity no longer wonders about the meaning of what is happening. Heidegger says this in *Der Spiegel:* what bothers him most about the world of technology is that "everything functions," and "that the functioning propels everything more and more toward further functioning," without anything happening to break off this game of "functioning" and leading to a questioning of the Being of technology.[62] Similarly, in "Overcoming Metaphysics": "The pain which must first be experienced and borne to the end is the insight and the knowledge that the lack of need is the supreme and hidden need which first necessitates in virtue of the most distant distance. Lack of need consists in believing that one has reality and what is real in one's grip and knows what truth is, without needing to know in what truth *presences*."[63] Thus technology, by endlessly supplying and intensifying the illusion of control, helps to cover over, to mask the withdrawal from Being (which Heidegger also calls "nihilism" in the sense of "abandonment far from Being"), a withdrawal of which it is nevertheless the product: forgetfulness settles into forgetfulness, the abandonment far from Being is abandoned to itself by thought which, entirely absorbed in "machining" the real, no longer even gives a glancing thought to the void in which the filling up of the universe with the objects of technology is merely the reverse side.

Thus the first task becomes, not just to bring about the technological completion of modernity, but "within its limits [to] help (*sic*) man as such to achieve a satisfactory relationship to the essence (*sic*) of technology" by showing the nihilism from which the technologizing of the world is inseparable: need we recall that it is in relation to the definition of this *help*—which brings man back from the absence of distress to distress—that Heidegger (in the next sentence) judged that he could say, *in 1966*, that "National Socialism did indeed go in that direction"?[64] That is, Nazism as antimodernism opposing modernity with the forgetfulness of what is operating in it.

The perceptible tension in the neoconservative attitude defining Heidegger's Nazism thus originates in a fundamental difficulty in his thinking. Chapter 4 discusses the philosophical significance of this difficulty and its indication of Heidegger's inability to conceive of a nonmetaphysical humanism.[65] For the time being, however, the main thing was to note that his support of the "conservative revolution" triggered by National Socialism surely referred less to the persistence in the "first" Heidegger of a vestige of the metaphysics of the will (hence, of humanism) than to an internal contradiction, from the beginning to the end, in an endeavor to have done with the will or with subjectivity, but one unable to think through the implications of what was thus attempted. Unable (fortunately) to dump subjectivity, but also unable to bestow on it any status other than the metaphysical, and thus of an obstruction to be eliminated, Heidegger then restricted himself to seeking a way out of this predicament in the effort actively to liquidate the subject, hence to turn the subject back on the subject so as to launch the resurgence of a world of tradition. A program as alarming as it is— and who would not agree?—of, at the very least, doubtful coherence.

The Forgetfulness of Modernity

These two aspects of Heidegger's assessment of Nazism bear witness to a serious *forgetfulness of modernity*. Whether we must get beyond democratic modernity to meet the unyielding demands of technology or must challenge political modernity, in the East or in the West, with the virtues of a tradition less forgetful of rootedness and better able to resist the uniformitizing of the world, *in both cases* the political resources of modernity, hence of democracy as well, are placed in abeyance: nothing can be expected of a political and cultural system revolving around the values of autonomy, a system to which the very decline of Europe is imputed.[66] Renouncing a quite different criticism of modernity, in which some attempt was made to hold it (as well as democracy) to the promises it has made and not kept, Heidegger devoted himself to a radical criticism of modernity, seeking the bases for his criticism outside modernity: under these circumstances, how could his moves not include an antimodern coiling back on the values of tradition and rootedness? What, in its complexity, Heidegger's assessment of Nazism thus reveals is at bottom the kind of dangers to which the hatred of the modern is exposed when it disallows the question of whether modernity may not itself be pluralistic and not reducible to what is made of it when it is seen as the reign of the "will to will," and when the coming of the führers is seen as the ineluctable outcome of the irruption of humanism.

4

Moderns and Antimoderns: Humanism in Question

Let us agree, however, that Heidegger's criticism of the modern world does not appeal to the French intelligentsia only because of the logic of the status and role of the intellectual in a democracy. However alluring the state of iconoclastic exteriority that is structurally involved in the role of the critical intellectual, it cannot explain the persuasiveness to honest intellectuals of Heidegger's depiction of the tragic destiny to which modern times seem by nature doomed.

The Tragic Side of Modernity

Truth to tell, this tragic side is intrinsic to the dynamics of democratic individualism.[1] On the one hand, this dynamics involves the gradual erosion of traditional religion and philosophy and also, it goes without saying, politics and history: in their desire for autonomy, in their real or fanciful plan of appropriating norms, individuals come to identify their freedom with making up their own rules and laws, a process that, at whatever level one looks at it, implies the gradual dissolution of reference points inherited from the past, or, which comes to the same thing, their continual overthrow. In parallel, on the other hand, a good many theoretical or existential questions, whose answers were self-evident in a traditional world, suddenly crop up anew in a democratic world, caught up as it is in a

never-ending whirl of autonomy. What in a traditional society was considered as a *rule* for all eternity becomes
problematical when viewed from the subjectivity whose
emergence Heidegger called the inauguration of modernity.

Modern times thus enter a seemingly diabolical circle,
for the two movements are mutually reinforcing: the
more questions spring up, the harder it is to respond to
them, ill-provided as we are with preestablished criteria;
as the world of tradition becomes less distinct, these criteria become less distinct, so more aspects of daily life as
well as intellectual life come under individual questioning.[2] Make no mistake, the tragic side of modernity is not
mere psychological torment but involves the ontological
essence of modern times and their indefinite subjectification of the world. If we add that this subjectification is not
limited to democratization (being subject to the principle
of autonomy and equality) but is coupled with the emergence of the world of pure technology and its consequent
transformation of culture into industrial mass culture, we
see how appealing and persuasive Heidegger's criticism of
this subjectification could be.

The Three Faces of Criticism
of the Modern World

The question, however, concerns less the *object* of the
criticism (who doesn't deplore chopping up movies with
commercials?) than the *purpose* of the criticism. The gap
between different aspects of criticism widens on the latter
point, not the former. Discussions of the infinite process
of modern subjectification point up the daunting problem
of the imposition of limits. As was suggested at the start
of this book, we have merely to consider such questions
as the ones now being debated in the various committees
of "sages" to see what problems are created by setting limits in a world no longer governed by tradition and in

which, consequently, the ever-increasing *immanence* of norms in the will of individuals seems to grant an infinite power to the plan for control of the self and the world: thus nothing seems a priori excluded from the domain of human *experimentation*.

Hence, a first possible face for the criticism of technological positivity: a criticism that, like Heidegger, identifies democracy as the subjectification of the world with its *inevitably* concomitant universe of technology and is oriented toward the stated or unstated ideal of a return to the premodern world of tradition. Here the criticism claims a basis in the *past*, a past thought of as embracing the norms of tradition and hierarchy: hence, there is nothing odd in the presence of this aspect of criticism in Heidegger (particularly in his writings from the 1930s) and in many of his students, orthodox or heterodox, when the democratic world and the world of technology seem successive faces of the same metaphysics and culture of the will.

A second face of this criticism, paradoxically very similar to the first one, may feed on a reference, not to this side of the modern world, but to the world to follow: paradoxically, it is on the basis of this divergence that Marxism and Heideggerianism may momentarily make common cause in attacking the despotic influence of "instrumental reason." Following Weber and Marx, Theodor Adorno and Max Horkheimer undertook to deconstruct that "administered world" (*verwaltete Welt*) whose essence is the mass culture to which they believed the sovereignty of technical reason inevitably conduces. Here, as in Heidegger, the administered world is none other than the worldly actualization of the metaphysics of subjectivity that culminates in Hegel's *Logic*. Unlike Heidegger, however, at least in the early stages of Critical Theory, criticism is pursued for the sake of a *future* thought of as objective reason, and not for the sake of some past. Mass culture is described more in terms of alienation than of control, more in terms of pseudorationality than perfect rationalization, for the Marx-inspired hope still persists of man's reconciliation with himself in a society without classes or contradictions. That the ideal of a radiant future has now faded is true not only in the French context but also in the German context of critical Marxism: in one of his last lectures, entitled "Kritische Theorie heute und gestern,"[3] Horkheimer explained how the Marxist ideal of objective reason gradually caved in as Critical Theory uncovered the intrinsically hegemonistic nature of rationality, including its claim to determine humanity's ends and hence to transcend a simple reflection on the means to which instrumental reason is limited.

Beyond their divergences, these two types of criticism still share the plan of deconstructing modernity that, whether in the name of tradition or utopia, is always condemned from a viewpoint exterior to it. We dare to confess that the status and legitimacy of this radical exteriority now seems to us ever more doubtful—which is why, in Horkheimer and especially Adorno, we would prefer to retain, for reasons to be examined, the idea of an *internal* criticism of the world of democracy, namely, the idea of a criticism that *at present* sees utopia within positivity, the nonplace inside the place, and to seek to draw out the subversive potentialities inscribed in the promises that the world of democracy has made but failed to honor.

For, whether done in the name of the past or the future, or even in a vacillation between these two positions—as we see not only in the later Horkheimer but also in a number of others, like Herbert Marcuse and Michel Foucault, who were drawn to both Marx and Heidegger—the disregarding of modern times is not without its problems.

One-Dimensional Thought

We have already stated how Heidegger's deconstruction of the metaphysics of subjectivity led him to lump liberalism and communism together in the same model, for both seemed to him two possible faces—one individualistic, one collectivistic—of the same world of technology.[4] And from this perspective Heideggerianism sounded the theme of a defense of Europe and particularly Germany as "the middle empire" opposed to the two essentially identical expressions of the will to will represented by the United States and the Soviet Union. Here we should cite in its entirety the passage from his 1935 *Introduction to Metaphysics* that we have already quoted in part:

> This Europe, which in its ruinous blindness is forever on the point of cutting its own throat, lies today in a great pincers, squeezed between Russia on one side and America on the other. *From a metaphysical point of view, Russia and America are the same: the same dreary technological frenzy, the same unrestricted organization of the average man.* At a time when the furthermost corner of the globe has been conquered by technology and opened to economic exploitation; when any incident whatever, regardless of where or when it occurs, can be communicated to the rest of the world at any desired speed; when the assassination of a king in France and a symphony concert in Tokyo can be "experienced" simultaneously; when time has ceased to be anything other than velocity, instantaneousness, and simultaneity, and time as history has vanished from the lives of all peoples; when a boxer is regarded as a nation's great man; when mass meetings attended by millions are looked on as a triumph—then, yes then, through all this turmoil a question still haunts us like a specter: What for?—Whither?—And what then?
>
> The spiritual decline of the earth is so far advanced that the nations are in danger of losing the

last bit of spiritual energy that makes it possible to
see the decline (taken in relation to the history of
[Being], and to appraise it as such. This simple observation has nothing to do with *Kulturpessimis-
mus*, and of course it has nothing to do with any sort
of optimism, either; for the darkening of the world,
the flight of the gods, the destruction of the earth,
the transformation of men into a mass, the hatred
and suspicion of everything free and creative, have
assumed such proportions throughout the earth that
such childish categories as pessimism and
optimism have long since become absurd."[5]

We have seen how these leitmotifs of Heidegger's
thinking in 1935 could tally—from the very foundation of
his philosophy (it is *from the metaphysical point of view*
that Russia and America are considered identical)—with
major aspects of the conservative revolution. What we
need to understand now is how a translation of this passage into the language of today may provide virtually in-
tact, for an important segment of a leftist intelligentsia
yearning for Marxism, the necessary intellectual instru-
ments for resuscitating the defunct figure of the critical
intellectual: Central Europe is no longer just Germany;
more extensive in both the West and the East (up to the
borders of the Soviet Union), it may again be the scene of
military activity that is both anti-American and anti-
Soviet. Finally realizing that Soviet bureaucracy was not a
degenerate worker state but a totalitarian and even strato-
cratic empire, the "Heideggerian left" can hang onto the
main thing: the idea that on the whole American pseudo-
liberalism is no better, that there are two faces of totalitarianism: George Orwell's *1984*, of course, but also Aldous
Huxley's *Brave New World*. The payoff is the chance to
condemn, no longer on the basis of Marx but of Heidegger,
the economic exploitation of the world, the false values of
the industrial culture (Bernard Tapie is the boxer Heideg-

ger is talking about, and Madonna draws the masses) in a decline where people are threatened with a loss of "life with thought" and thus with a descent into a human herding together that is called "barbarism" from the view-point of a radical exteriority beyond optimism or pessimism.

Like Marxism in other times, this neo-Heideggerianism still has the advantage of what Karl Popper called "verificationism"; it is enough to open the news-paper, to look at television, or to listen to the radio, to find the myriad signs and symptoms that confirm a thesis that nothing, really, could falsify. That the media *also* have an informative role, that the birth of ephemeral stars *also* means a decrease in master thinkers and messianic ideologies, that conflicts are settled to a degree, or that the political culture become more democratic: so many objections that can be dismissed with a flick of the hand, so many signs of a freedom that an impeccably Heideggerian logic finds only too easy to prove inauthentic, thoroughly caught up as it is in the world of technology and enframing.

The debate cannot be settled by *facts:* in deciding be-tween essentially unfalsifiable visions of the world, it is of no avail to set the empirical against the empirical. The most one can do is examine their internal coherence and subsequent effects.

From this viewpoint, it is first of all clear, as we have noted, that this criticism of technology as the global con-cretization of an idea of man as *consciousness* and *will* implies, like it or not, a deconstruction of democratic rea-son and hence, in some sense, of humanism. It is also clear, however, that Heidegger's thinking, even fixed up this way, continues in some odd way to misfire because of its one-dimensionality. Just as, on the strictly philosophi-cal level, it leads to lumping the various facets of modern subjectivity together in a shapeless mass and to judging that the progression from Descartes to Kant to Nietzsche is linear and in fact inevitable; just as, on the political level, it leads to the brutal inclusion of American liberalism *in the same category* with Stalinist totalitarianism. Now this is no mere matter of taste: anyone has the right to loathe rock concerts, Disney World, and California. Nonetheless, no one may—Hannah Arendt and Leo Strauss, who lived in the United States, did not make this mistake—identify, in the name of a higher authority, the barbarism of the Soviet gulags with the depravities of a Western society whose extraordinary political, social, and cultural complexity allows areas of freedom that it would be wholly unwarranted to judge a priori as mere fringes or remnants of a world in decline.

It is probably just as wrongheaded to conflate the essences of American democracy and totalitarianism as to declare, as did Heidegger—*for the same reasons and in accordance with the same assessment of technology*—that "motorized agriculture is ... in essence the same thing as the manufacture of corpses in the gas chambers and extermination camps, the same thing as the blockading and starvation of nations, the same thing as the manufacture of hydrogen bombs." Simply this: if that is so, what is it *not* to be the same thing? If motorized agriculture is identical with the gas chambers, we ask, with no intent to be ironical: what is to prevent a gradual chain of equivalences from holding Adolf Hitler, Joseph Stalin, and Yves Mourousi to be the three kings of contemporary barbarism?[6]

The ultimate goal of this one-dimensional reading of modern times is a criticism of humanism and democracy *as such*. In this regard, it is with great coherence that Philippe Lacoue-Labarthe, a dissident but still strict Heideggerian on this point, expresses in the same gesture his alignment with the figure of the critical intellectual and his hatred of democracy.:

Heidegger overestimated Nazism and probably figured what was on its way before 1933 in cost-benefit

terms, but to which he was still resolutely opposed:
anti-Semitism, ideology (the "politicized science"),
precipitous brutality. But I would add: who, whether
he was of "the right" or "the left," was not taken
in by the spectacle of the unprecedented world-
historic mutation of which this century was the
stage and by the apparent radicalness of the revolutionary proposals? And in the name of what would
he have not been taken in? "In the name of democracy"? Let's leave that to Raymond Aron, that is,
to the official idea of capitalism (of full-blown nihilism, for which everything *has a price*). But those
who were great of their kind? At random: Knut
Hamsun, Gottfried Benn, Ezra Pound, Maurice
Blanchot, Pierre Drieu La Rochelle, and Robert
Brasillach (I also include Louis-Ferdinand Céline,
though his writing seems to me overrated), or, on the
other side, Walter Benjamin, Bertolt Brecht, Georges
Bataille, André Malraux (I also include Sartre, of
whose moral authenticity there is no doubt). What
did the old world offer them to parry the intrusions
of the self-styled "new world"? From this angle and
all things considered, Heidegger's merit, incalculable *today*, is to have yielded for only ten months
to this *two-faced* illusion of "new times." [7]

Here, Lacoue-Labarthe's incalculable merit is to betray
in a few lines the unhappily inevitable logic of new-look
Heideggerianism. Beyond the judgment of Raymond
Aron, the ritualistic conformism of the critical intellectual, we note, in no particular order: (1) "who thinks
greatly must err greatly," and the more-than-human error
becomes a merit when committed in the name of a position of exteriority relative to the old world, a veritable
shibboleth of the critical intellectual; (2) the thinker of
the left may go on calmly identifying democracy with the
superstructure of capital and the media intellectuals with
the hirelings of imperialism; (3) consistent with Heideg-

ger's "Letter on Humanism," nihilism, i.e., completed metaphysics, is confounded with ethics, since "any valorization is subjectification"; and (4) despite all, for good measure he reduces to "ten months" an involvement that we now know was in some sense never renounced.

Like Marxism, which also hastened to condemn bourgeois ideology in all modern forms of subjectivity and for this reason also disregarded any difference between human rights and capitalism, between capitalism and fascism, between fascism and Nazism as the ultimate stage of imperialism, Heideggerianism thus managed to lump the political and the philosophical forms of subjectivity in the same category. Everything is "humanism": the Enlightenment and romanticism, individualism and collectivism, capitalism and fascism, Nazism and Stalinism. Provided one protects the position of the critical intellectual endangered by the waning of Marxism, the idea that nothing "has a price" has come to mean, strangely, that everything is six of one and a half dozen of another.

The Humanisms

Faced with this new form of one-dimensionality, we badly need to differentiate between the various faces of humanism, so that a remark of the type "Nazism is a humanism" can be seen to be preposterous.

On the question of the definition (or the absence of definition) of man's humanity and hence of his possible differentiation from animality and thinghood, in its core modern thought includes three competing traditions: (1) the thematization of the Enlightenment in the critical philosophy of Rousseau, Kant, and Fichte; (2) the romantic deconstruction of the Enlightenment, whose repercussions are discernible in Hegelianism; and (3) phenomenology. These three traditions are intricately articulated, for criticism and phenomenology are jointly opposed to the romantic image of man but diverge on the crucial question of the status of subjectivity.

The Romantic Critique of Enlightenment Humanism

In many ways, Heidegger's deconstruction of the metaphysics of subjectivity was prefigured in the romantic criticism of the Enlightenment.[8] This point is that what the romantics condemned in the philosophes' ideology is the claim of subjectivity, meaning consciousness and the desire to refashion the world by wiping clean the slate of tradition. Against the illusions of the tabula rasa, in which the subject (the individual or the people) is viewed as the foundation, the romantics endeavored to think of the various aspects of culture—philosophy, religion, law, language, and so forth—as products of *Life*. And it was by reference to this concept of Life that the romantics meant to go beyond a major opposition in the philosophy of the Enlightenment: the opposition between natural rights (the transcendent standard that the philosophes saw as rational right) and positive rights, between the ought and the is.

To grasp the significance and stakes of what thus appears to be a synthesis for resolving the question of man's *humanitas*, we need to specify what the romantics meant by Life. Without embarking on a detailed account of the history of this idea from Kant's *Critique of Judgment* to Schelling's early work on the philosophy of nature, we can grasp the synthetic function of the concept when we see how the living creature is a whole that both transcends and is immanent in its parts: it transcends because it does not necessarily stop existing when one of its parts, an organ, is injured or even destroyed, but, on the contrary, it spontaneously initiates reproductive or compensatory processes; it is immanent, however, since it exists nowhere else than as embodied in its parts. We can then see the parallelism with the question of rights: in the tradition of the philosophes, natural right contrasts with positive right as transcendence contrasts with immanence: natural right has a claim to universality in the face of a positive right which is always a particular right that is historically and geographically located in the framework of a particular *nation*.

The romantics' concept of Life enabled them to get beyond this contrast so typical of the philosophy of human rights: just as real life is a union of soul and body, and hence, if you will, of the universal and of the particular, of intelligence and sensibility (when one member in these pairs is taken away, the immediate result is death), so the true life of a people must be a union of natural right and positive right—a reconciliation of transcendence and immanence. This is the way Friedrich Karl von Savigny, the greatest romantic philosopher of rights, tried to transcend the opposition between universalism and relativism while escaping the charge of conservatism: the romantic respect for tradition does not necessarily take the form of conservatism when we see that every living creature, the body politic, the *Volksgeist*, goes through a birth and a death. The juridical task is not so much to preserve or defend tradition at any cost as it is to determine and set forth what is in the order of life, as Savigny plainly iterated in his 1814 "On the Vocation of our Age for Legislation and Jurisprudence": "The rigorous historical method . . . does not consist in unconditionally demanding the preservation of whatever matter is given . . . , its effort is rather to analyze the given material down to its roots so as to discover its organic principle, by which what is still living will automatically separate itself from what is dead."[9] Thanks to this method, "the living connection with the original conditions of peoples can be preserved," the loss of this connection having "the effect of ripping out from a people the finest part of its spiritual life."

The implications of this vitalistic ontology are many.

To address just the question of interest here, the question of humanism, romanticism implies a radical change in the idea of individuality. In the final analysis, the philosophy of the Enlightenment confounded the individual with the personality (only the individual is a person). For the romantics, however true individuality could only mean the national community, which is authentically alive only when it reconciles the universal (the social whole) with the particular (which the Enlightenment still called the individual)—the ideology of human rights thus appearing not only as "egoistic" (in the sense Marx used the term in his critique of French declarations of the rights of man), but as a *dead abstraction*.

Vitalistic nationalism thus involves the rejection of both individualism and the transcendence of norms, the features by which the romantic critique of the Enlightenment joins with the foremost themes of French counter-revolutionary thought, notably the celebrated formula of Joseph de Maistre, which is worth quoting: "The Constitution of 1795, like its predecessors, was made for *man*. But there is no such thing as *man* in the world. In my lifetime I have seen Frenchmen, Italians, Russians, etc.; thanks to Montesquieu, I even know that *one can be Persian*. But as for *man*, I declare that I have never in my life met him; if he exists, he is unknown to me." [10]

One is persuaded that this criticism of abstract humanism became the basic feature of the counterrevolution when one reads the following passage from Louis de Bonald's *Discours préliminaire à la législation primitive:* "The Christians had professed that power comes from God. . . . In power John Wycliffe sees only man. . . . From there follow as necessary consequences the doctrines of conventional and conditional power of Thomas Hobbes and John Locke, Jean-Jacques Rousseau's *Social Contract*, Pierre Jurieu's *Souveraineté Populaire*, and so forth. Power came only from man; to be legitimate, it must be constituted and exercised according to certain conditions imposed by man, to which conditions it could, in case of violation, be restored by the force of man; for that is at bottom the opinion of the political writers of the sixteenth century and the ones that followed, an opinion developed then and since, sometimes modified in many writings, and supported in our own day by great and terrible examples."

In their attempt to lend some credibility to the claim that Nazism is a humanism, Derrida and his followers now tend to favor, through a strange inversion of word meaning, the idea that humanism features the plan of giving man a definition and thus of creating an anthropology that ends up with a racist definition of the authentic man as an Aryan. One of the chief interests in the quarrel between romanticism and the philosophes of the Enlightenment is to remind us, since there is a need for it, that it was counterrevolutionary romanticism that, in a radical rejection of abstract humanism, defined man as merely a member of a national community, as a secondary reality, as a simple accident. And it is just as evident in the "Declaration of the Rights of Man" that there burst onto the political scene Kant's and Rousseau's essential idea that, on the contrary, man is characterized by his capacity to transcend any particular definition, to wrench free of historical, biological, and national determinations in order to enter into communication with other men. This is the meaning of that abstract humanism that de Maistre and de Bonald, along with Savigny and Müller, denounced in the various constitutions born of the French Revolution. This point deserves some amplification.

The Phenomenological and Criticist Critiques of Romanticism

Connections have often been found between Heidegger's thinking and German romanticism. Heidegger's deconstruction of the metaphysics of subjectivity echoes the romantic criticism of abstract humanism on many points. The analogy, however, is somewhat misleading. For Heidegger was attacking subjectivity in the name of a quite different conception of man, one implying a radical deconstruction of romantic vitalism, which is reduced to one simple figure of modern metaphysics. And in this branch of his work, which gets him away from romanticism, we cannot deny that, through Husserl's phenomenology, Heidegger echoes the fundamental themes of criticism.

With regard to the definition of man, Heidegger fully understood the meaning and applicability of Husserl's critique of psychologism and, more generally, of any form of vitalism and historicism. Husserl's point is quite clear: if psychology or history or life are thought of as codes that entirely determine human behavior, then there is no distinction between humanity and animality, or even between humanity and thinghood. Man is then a simple machine whose actions, reduced to pure movements, could in principle be wholly predictable. Thus man's *humanitas* or *Eigentlichkeit* lies in his capacity to wrench free of his determinations (which Kant called "freedom," Husserl "transcendence," Sartre "existence," Heidegger "eksistence," and Arendt "action") in nothingness understood as the absence of definability by a general code.

Heidegger expands on this thesis at some length, and quite soundly, in his "Letter on Humanism": "What man is—or, as it is called in the traditional language of metaphysics, the 'essence' of man—lies in his eksistence"[11]—hence, for Heidegger, in his ability to wrench free of the world of beings, to transcend it, to ask the question for thinking, the question of Being. Animals are certainly living creatures and not things, but "in any case, living creatures are what they are without standing outside their Being as such and within the truth of Being."[12]

Hence Heidegger had to make two distinctions: first

the distinction between animals—who are "without a world" because they are incapable of wrenching free of the domination of a vital instinctual code—and men, who are Da-sein, i.e., literally the "there" of Being, the opening to Being, and thus are not wedded to beings in the machinelike and imperious quest for the satisfaction of vital needs; and on the other hand, the distinction, within humanity, between men who achieve authenticity, "thought," and those who demean themselves in a reifying, i.e., codifying, world of mere absorption. Arendt repeated this theme in much of her critique of totalitarian ideologies that also reify man, thus nullifying any possible "action" by reducing it to a simple plaything of nature (like race) or history (like class). Using the same logic, Arendt denounced the dangers of the "social question," of that "socialization" in which modern man sees his freedom of action constantly threatened by society's singular powers of codification.

It needs to be emphasized that this Husserlian legacy greatly inspired Sartre when, contrary to what Heidegger asserts,[13] in "Existentialism is a Humanism," he made a distinction between humanity and thinghood:

> Let us consider some object that is manufactured, for example, a book or a paper cutter: here is an object which has been made by an artisan whose inspiration came from a concept. . . . Thus, the paper cutter is at once an object produced in a certain way and, on the other hand, one having a specific use; and one cannot postulate a man who produces a paper cutter but does not know what it is used for. Therefore let us say that, for the paper cutter, essence—that is, the ensemble of both the production routines and the properties which enable it to be both produced and defined—precedes existence. Thus, the presence of the paper cutter or book in front of me is determined. Therefore, we have here a

technical view of the world whereby it can be said
that production precedes existence.[14]

In short, to parody Heidegger: "Things are what they are";
they have a definition, an essence that they cannot escape.
And Sartre criticizes theology and traditional philosophy
for conceiving of man as a fabricated object and, correspondingly, of God as a "superior sort of artisan." In this
vision of the world, human freedom vanishes; man finds
himself prisoner to a nature, assigned an end or a model
he can no more evade than can the paper cutter: here, "the
concept of man in the mind of God is comparable to the
concept of a paper cutter in the mind of the manufac-
turer." Authentic humanism, however, is characterized by
the idea that "there is at least one creature in whom existence precedes essence, a creature that exists before being
definable, and that this creature is man . . . if man as existentialism conceives of him is not definable, that is because he is at first nothing."[15]

It is apropos to note that in the name of this humanism
Sartre can denounce sexism as an ideology that reduces
the woman's humanity to purely natural determinations,
and Marxist sociologism as one that reduces the human
being to purely historical determinations. Jean Beaufret
has noted that this existential critique conforms not only
to the tradition of Husserl's phenomenology but also Heidegger's when, repeating Sartre's theses in *Introduction
aux philosophies de l'existence*, he says: "Can there be
dignity without freedom? For finally, if the bourgeoisie,
having unknowingly 'forged the weapons of its own
death,' 'produces,' through excess, 'the men who will
wield these weapons,' by the same necessity that the apple
tree produces apples, then however much I call that necessity *dialectics* and contrast it with simple mechanical necessity, will it be any the less necessity? And in the final
analysis, before the revolution that will come from their
mass, won't the proletariat have the fundamental inno-

cence of the tree before its fruits: 'I have no choice, it's stronger than I'?"[16]

These themes are well-known and quite sound. *What is too often overlooked, however, is that, far from breaking with the philosophy of the Enlightenment, this phenomenological or existentialist conception of humanism harks back beyond romanticism to the chief theses of Rousseau, Kant, and Fichte on man's humanity.* Rousseau dwells on it at considerable length in his *Discourse on the Origin of Inequality:* human freedom is revealed in the ability to break free from nature, that is, if you will, through the absence of a definition or essence—and therein lies the distinguishing property of man: "nature alone does everything in the operations of a beast, whereas man contributes to his operation by being a free agent. The former chooses or rejects by instinct and the latter by an act of freedom, *so that a beast cannot deviate from the rule that is prescribed to it even when it would be advantageous for it to do so, and a man deviates from it often to his detriment.*" (Jean-Jacques Rousseau, *The First and Second Discourses,* trans. Roger D. Masters and Judith R. Masters [New York: St. Martin's Press, 1964], p. 113). Thus the animal may starve to death in the presence of food that it is not programmed to consume instinctively, while man may drink himself to death. The example here has symbolic value: it means that man alone is capable of wrenching free, as Arendt said, of the cycle of life. The true difference between man and animal, that "about which there can be no dispute: the faculty of self-perfection. . . . By contrast, an animal is at the end of a few months what it will be all its life; and its species is at the end of a thousand years what it was the first year of that thousand" (Rousseau, *Discourse on Inequality,* pp. 114–15).

Owing to this unique capacity not to be a prisoner of natural determinations, only man comes up against the formidable problem of individual history (education) and collective history (politics). "Societies" of bees or ants are societies with no history, and for most animals, the reflexes needed for survival come into play immediately upon birth. This is also the source—and phenomenology may have grasped this better than any other contemporary philosophy—of man's possible fall into inauthenticity, which here means forgetting his own transcendence, that negation of freedom involved in acting as though one were a creature, as though nature or history could become our codes.

This conception of man demanded that Rousseau approach in rejuvenated terms what we now call the question of racism. If man is perfectibility, if perfectibility is the nullification of nature and history—and thus of true historicity—and if this historicity is that of a wrenching free of natural or social determinations, how are we to think of those primitive societies that seem, like societies of bees and ants, to lack the distinctively human dimension, bound as they are to the strictly repetitive order of tradition? Rousseau's answer is merely sketched in the *Discourse:* "Savage man, by nature committed to instinct alone, or rather compensated for the instinct he perhaps lacks by faculties capable of substituting for it at first, and then of raising him far above nature, will therefore begin with purely animal functions" (Rousseau, *Discourse on Inequality,* p. 115).

It would be hard to overstate the importance of this passage. Here Rousseau sketches, in direct connection with a conception of man as perfectibility or a nothingness, the first democratic conception philosophically based on the savage world: if the savage *seems* not yet properly human, it is not, for Rousseau, because he occupies a lower place than humanity in the hierarchy of creatures, intermediate, as it were, between humanity and animality, and is literally "subhuman" (*Unter-Mensch*). Although his lack of historicity makes him akin to the animal, savage man is in no way an animal—he is guided not by an instinctual code but by his faculties of pity and self-love, which come to make up for the absence of instinct and which, though still much underdeveloped, bear in the bud the mark of infinite freedom. And this area of freedom is thus confounded with the infinite distancing from nature typified by the processes of education and politics.

No doubt there still exists the possibility of a Eurocentrist distinction between savage and civilized man; it remains true—and this is the main point—that Rousseau abolishes this distinction *in principle* so that humanity appears as truly *one*. Even if the savage world were downgraded in relation to Europe (which in Rousseau is in no way obvious), that world would not be natural but human and hence must be respected through a logic of *inclusion*, and not of *exclusion*.

It was Kant who gave a fully coherent vision of history that underlies this new humanism, according to which the ideal of universal communication is not an imposed model but the rigorous consequence of the definition of man as a nothingness; man, be he European or other, may enter into communication with other cultures and thus attain universality by wrenching himself from the particularity of national identities. Complementarily, it becomes in principle impossible to judge and condemn men for what they *are* (crime against humanity), but it is in what they *do* that they are, may we say, permitted to *err*. Therefore the ultimate goal of human action cannot be happiness; in the quest for happiness, man remains subject to the cycle of life, and it is only, as paragraph 83 of the *Critique of Judgment* shows, to the extent that he transcends the world of life that man may be regarded as an end in himself. Thus, echoing Rousseau's writings, these passages from Kant and Fichte:

Kant: "Animals are by their instinct all that they can ever be; some other reason has provided everything for them at the outset. . . . Man needs nurture and culture [*Bildung*]. These, as far as we know, no animal needs. . . ."[17]

Fichte: "All animals are perfect and complete; man, however, is merely suggested. . . . Every animal *is* what it is; man alone is originally nothing at all. What man is to be, he must become. . . ."[18]

Thus, our account of the existence of primitive peoples seemingly ensnared in naturality must involve purely historical criteria and not criteria that are natural or accidental, and essential. Though mythical, Kant's explanation deserves serious consideration. As Alexis Philonenko has luminously demonstrated,[19] eighteenth-century philosophy saw the savage among savages as having two faces: that of the Greenlander half-frozen in the glacial wastes of the North Pole, and the symmetrical one of the indigene of the earthly paradise of the South Seas. In rebutting the traditional racist argument that the Greenlander or West Indian was "subhuman," Kant argued that both of them were rightful members of the historical human world thought of as perfectibility. If the tribes to the north and south have not fully wrenched free of nature and entered into historicity, the reason is that the natural environment is either too hostile or too benign: why should the West Indian proceed to work and thus break himself free of nature when the nature around him is paradise? The case of the Greenlander is a bit more delicate. While we can appreciate man's reason for living in the South Seas, the choice of the North Pole is perplexing. So Kant studied history to understand how certain tribes that had been defeated in war were forced to seek exile in these hostile regions. Once again, the interpretation is mythical but keeps its symbolic value by explaining the plurality of cultures on a basis other than nature.

It may, and no doubt will, be said that this conception of historicity could also serve as a basis for ethnocentrism. It is in this sense that Derrida in *Of Spirit* devotes the important note, which we have already encountered, to the Eurocentrist ideology of which the thematics of human rights would be the bearer. And in this connection he cites the following passage from Husserl's "Crisis of European Humanity": "In the spiritual sense, the English dominions, the United States and so on, plainly belong to Europe, but not the Eskimos or the Indians in traveling zoos or the gypsies who permanently roam all over Europe."[20] Derrida suggests that this joint reference to the spirit and Europe would play "a major, organizing role in the transcendental teleology of reason as Eurocentric humanism," and in support he quotes another passage from Husserl: "just as man, and even the Papuan, represents a new stage in animality in contrast to the animals, so philosophical reason represents a new stage in humanity and in its reason" (quoted in Jacques Derrida, *Origin of Geometry*, trans. John P. Leavey, Jr. [Brighton: Harvester Press, 1978], p. 162). Hence, Derrida judges, the "terrible contaminations" attendant on the plan of democratic humanism: by giving man a *spiritual* definition, humanism not only implies the differentiation of humans from other beings (animals, things) but also demands that men be divided into the authentic and the inauthentic, depending on whether or not they embody what is to be the distinguishing property of man (in Husserl's case, spirituality or reason). The stakes of the argument are all too clear: Derrida is of course arguing against the critics of antihumanism that there is a fine line between humanism and Eurocentrist, colonialist racism, a line that is all the more tenuous owing to the manifest connection between the spiritualistic definition of man and an attitude of exclusion. Hence Derrida's conclusion: these two sentences of Husserl's and the humanistic ideology they strenuously convey may, all things considered, be "worse" than Heidegger's involvement with the Nazis (Derrida, *Of Spirit*, p. 122).

A serious mistake, nonetheless. Consistent with Husserl's critique of psychologism, spirituality does not mean for him man's ability not to be wedded to naturality. And he affirms the superiority of Europeans over Papuans only relative to this scale of values. Recent developments in anthropology, particularly the studies of Claude Lévi-Strauss and Pierre Clastres, have disencumbered us of the illusion that the culture of savages is closer to nature than is European civilization. Now we know—but it must be recalled that this knowledge was hard to come by in Husserl's day and harder yet in Kant's—that the difference between cultures cannot be nonchalantly measured with the yardstick of a teleological history of humanity. This argument, sound though it is, should not leave us free to gloss over the fundamental difference that, despite appearances, separates Kant and Husserl from Hegel or Marx: the point is not that Husserl or Kant valorized European culture (which is, after all, far from being illegitimate), but that they considered history, in whatever place and in whatever people it occurs, as a history of freedom that transcends natural and social determinations. Thus for them it is purely a question of *fact* whether this or that people, or this or that culture, symbolizes this strictly human capacity better than some other. There is in this no evolutionism of *principle*. However, in the various metaphysics of history, it is not through freedom but by necessity—by that the necessity of their social nature, so to speak—that peoples are destined to embody a particular world-historical determinacy, and except by accident (one thinks of Russia, which disproved the general thesis that the revolution would take place in the most highly developed countries, hence in Western Europe), they cannot get away from this law of history. On closer inspection, Husserl's writings are not as offensive as they seem from a cursory and, in fact, inimical reading: building on the idea that culture is a wrenching free of nature and is thus the work of freedom, Husserl is not laying the groundwork for colonialism but rather for the outlook—which now de-

fines authentic third-worldism, freed of the illusions of
ideologies that are destructive of national identity—in
which aid to the third world is seen not as charity but as
the learning of freedom. In this respect, militant third-
worldism has long been unable to get completely free of
the colonialist illusions it wanted to reverse, and charity,
though no doubt more humane, has been worth little
more than tutelary paternalism.

Phenomenology and Criticism: The Point of Cleavage

The source of the profound divergence between critical
philosophy and Heideggerian phenomenology lies else-
where. Despite Derrida's efforts, it is not clear, after all,
how superior to Husserl in this respect a thinker was who
saw the fate of humanity lying not just with Europe, but
within Europe, with Germany alone.

Through the agency of Husserl, phenomenology is akin
to the inspiration of critical philosophy: nothing decisive
separates Heidegger from Kant, or Arendt from Husserl, in
the designation of the distinguishing property of man as
nothing or as ek-sistence. The real question is quite different. It is whether—*once it is admitted, against the romantics, that ek-sistence is the distinguishing property
of man*—we should think of the capacity to wrench oneself free of natural or social codes as an act of conscious
volition (virtue in Kant's sense) or as what Heidegger
called *Ereignis,* by which he meant not only a wrenching
free of naturality but a wrenching that in man as Dasein
depends on Being and hence takes place in a different setting from the subjective faculties. In the first case, the
wrenching free from naturality is thought to be based on
the subject's free decision; in the other case, man is un-
wittingly, so to speak, wrenched from this naturality—in
a view of subjectivity reminiscent of the romantic theory

of genius; the genius rises above natural or social codes to create a work of shimmering autonomy and remarkable uniqueness that is the objective sign of this transcendence; but the genius is creative because he does this quite *unconsciously*, without having explicitly *willed* or totally *foreseen* it.

The stakes of this fundamental divergence should not be concealed. Each of the two positions raises commensurate problems. If we admit that we can wrench ourselves from naturality through a free and conscious decision, how do we avoid falling into what Heidegger rightly impugns as the illusions of the metaphysics of subjectivity? How can we avoid once again making the subject, understood as consciousness and will, the ultimate foundation of human actions—and thus forgetful of Being (of the invisible, of the unconscious, and so on)? Why can't we also see, however, that if we circumvent this fall into metaphysics by making this wrenching an *Ereignis* (Heidegger) or "action" in Arendt's sense, hence an act that is required of man, rather than one by which he decides, we risk foundering in a new historicism? Man is certainly not determined by the code of a causalistic history, as is supposed by traditional sociologism and psychologism; he is nonetheless imprisoned by a code, if only the "history of Being," that is just as profound: what does it really matter whether man is required by causality or Being if in either case he is deprived of the act that forms his distinguishing property and is thereby left to "destiny," if only the "destiny of Being"? In this respect doesn't phenomenology, which has long kept its distance from romanticism, risk—as, moreover, seems indicated by Heidegger's German nationalism, which was once that of the romantics— repudiating its criticist ancestry, and linking up with the idea that history is our code? Whether Germany is invested with the mission of salvation because of its *Volksgeist* or through the effect of a history of Being in which it takes up the extinguished torch of the Greek tradition, isn't phenomenology only minimally different from criticism?

Let's take a further look into the problems with phenomenology.[21] At times it has been believed that one could show that Arendt's category of action,[22] through which man breaks free of the natural attitude born of manufacturing and of socialization, would be an adequate basis on which to construct not only a sound philosophy of human rights but also a judgment valorizing the modern (egalitarian) world over the ancient (hierarchical) world. The argument is as follows: certainly our understanding of the world is established historically and symbolically, i.e., taken in a certain historical opening that constitutes us as essentially modern, wedded as we are to the values of equality. This proposal, which grants a certain role to tradition, is nonetheless historicist. From this perspective, the answer must be negative. It would have to be said that in this established modern democratic order, appearance and the established sense of what appears do not coincide. This noncoincidence would then involve the fact that we as human beings are not mirrors that automatically reflect the order to which we belong: we can wrench free from the natural attitude to wonder about the meaning of the codes or orders we live with. Unlike what held for the romantics, there would thus be no historicism in the phenomenological conception of tradition.

If this analysis is correct, the conclusion unfortunately goes beyond what is contained in the premises. It falls short on the two essential features separating the phenomenological and the criticist conceptions of action, though both are based on a common definition of man as transcendence.

1. First, despite the complexity of the question, it is clear that the concept of action can truly circumvent historicism only if we introduce some element of volition in the act of transcendence. If man is destined by Being to

wonder about the meaning of the political order around him, his code is Being, and traditional thinking overrides the idea of ek-sistence.

2. Granted that there is no important difference between the history of Being and the history of freedom, between the wrenching free thought of as a decision and the wrenching free thought of as the destiny of Being, for in both cases, in Kant as well as in Heidegger and Arendt, we are explicitly referred to mystery and the incomprehensible (the mystery of the will, the mystery of Being), a second question remains wholly unanswered: if, as Heidegger correctly wrote in his "Letter on Humanism," any valorization is a subjectification in that the subject sets itself up as a critical authority for evaluating the positivity of what is, it is indeed necessary that a minimum of subjectivity be reintroduced so that from the simple *comprehension* of democratic meanings one can decide on their *valorization* relative to the hierarchical world of tradition.

Let us go further. Even if we grant that the subject does not simply mirror the order in which it lives, if we admit that it is opening or transcendence, it must still refer to an idea of subjectivity, meaning reflection, so that the idea of the subject as opening (authenticity, "life with thought") is valorized rather than the reification of the subject as a mirror (inauthenticity).

Whatever is true of this debate, which, it will be readily agreed, here remains open, one thing is still certain. Heidegger is not close to Nazism because he remained a prisoner of humanism, nor because of his deliberations about authenticity and the distinguishing property of man. For Heidegger, the distinguishing property of man is always transcendence, and on the contrary, it was in the name of this transcendence and thus because he was still a humanist that Heidegger could criticize the biologizing reifications of Nazi anti-Semitism. More generally, it is very much in the name of humanism thus understood, in the name of that strictly human capacity to wrench oneself free of natural determinations, that a criticism of the racist imagination (in the Lacanian sense) is possible. When, however, Heidegger makes the destiny of Being the destiny of man, when he thus returns to the antihumanist idea of a traditional code (if only that of the history of Being), he founders in inauthenticity, and his fall makes possible the return of the nationalistic myth and the fanatical hatred of modernity.

Conclusion

The problems that the phenomenological tradition faces in thinking about the question of the deconstructed subject show up at three levels:

1. Impossible to set up in the framework of phenomenology, the valorization or devalorization of what exists is always surreptitiously reintroduced, like the return of something repressed: for Heidegger himself, the world of technology ought not strictly be devalorized in relation to an ideal of life with thought, since this world is one destiny of Being. Nevertheless, no one can seriously deny that Heidegger took a *critical* attitude toward the modern world. But just like valorization or devalorization, criticism is a specifically modern idea, for it demands that the subject be set up as the authority in evaluation. Thus, in phenomenology, the viewpoint of subjectivity, if unchecked, continually threatens to take the form of a pure decisionism that is in essence radically excluded from the sphere of discussion.

2. If it is supposed that the idea of the history of Being can be made perfectly coherent, thus completely eliminating the viewpoint of the will underlying any moral vision of the world, phenomenology then begins to look like neoromanticism, a traditionalism of Being. And it is this perspective that for Heidegger justifies the selection of the German nation as the saving people, recreating tradi-

tion against the process of infinite uprooting that, in both the East and the West, defines modernity.

3. Unfortunately, the phenomenological covering up of the question of the subject conjoins these two difficulties; as a criticism of the modern world, it must be both voluntarist (because it is critical) and antivoluntarist (because it is antimodern), and thus both modern and antimodern: that is why it always risks being seduced by the various political faces of neoconservatism.

Heidegger was satisfied to confess that his involvement with Nazism was "a big blunder." That was nicely put. But the enigmas and errant ways of democracy call for much more in the philosopher than hatred or anguish.

Notes

Introduction

1. Luc Ferry and Alain Renaut, *French Philosophy of the Sixties: An Essay on Antihumanism*, trans. Mary Schnackenberg (Amherst, Mass.: University of Massachusetts Press, 1990).

2. Parts of this work can be found in Luc Ferry and Alain Renaut, *Système et critique, essai sur la critique de la raison dans la pensée contemporaine* (Brussels: Ousia, 1985).

3. Philippe Lacoue-Labarthe, *La Fiction du politique: Heidegger, l'art et la politique* (Paris: Christian Bourgois, 1987), p. 81.

4. Jacques Derrida, *Of Spirit: Heidegger and the Question*, trans. Geoffrey Bennington and Rachel Bowlby (Chicago: University of Chicago Press, 1989), p. 66. We discuss these warnings of Derrida's in chapter 3.

5. Victor Farias, *Heidegger and Nazism*, edited by Joseph Margolis and Tom Rockmore; translation from French by Paul Burrell and from the German by Gabriel R. Ricci (Philadelphia: Temple University Press, 1989). First published in 1987 as *Heidegger et le nazisme*.

6. Jean-Paul Sartre, *Search for a Method*, trans. Hazel E. Barnes (New York: Alfred A. Knopf, 1967), p. 15, n. 1.

7. The expression is Eric Weil's, who made it the title of his article in *Temps modernes* (3 [1947–48]: 128–38) at the time of the first great debate about Heidegger's Nazism, shortly after the Liberation.

8. Word of the French reaction even reached Germany. Primarily because of the much fainter interest in Heidegger there,

at first scant attention was paid to Farias's book. So the book first appeared in a French translation before being accepted by the German publisher Fischer. On the Germans' surprise at the book's reception in France, see *Der Spiegel* 48 (1987) and an article by Hans Georg Gadamer in *le Nouvel Observateur* (22 October 1988).

9. It began with "Entretien avec Martin Heidegger" by Maurice de Gandillac and "Visite à Martin Heidegger" of Frédéric de Towarnicki, *Temps modernes* 1 (1945–46): 713–16, 717–24. The real dispute, however, was between Karl Löwith ("Les implication politiques de la philosophie de l'existence chez Heidegger," *Temps modernes* 2 [1946]: 346–60) and Alphonse de Waelhens, the future cotranslator of one part of Heidegger's *Being and Time* ("Le philosophie de Heidegger et le nazisme," *Temps modernes* 3 [1947–48]: 115–27). In issue 3, de Waelhens's defense of Heidegger was accompanied by a fresh attack, this time by Eric Weil: "Le cas Heidegger," (pp. 128–38). Löwith and de Waelhens concluded the debate by exchanging a "Réponse à M. de Waelhens" and "Réponse à cette réponse," *Temps modernes* 4 (1948): 370–73, 374–77.

10. Thus, for example, de Waelhens, *Temps modernes* 3, p. 115: "We in no way mean to judge Heidegger's *personal* attitude toward National Socialism. All that matters to us is whether Heidegger's philosophy is intrinsically connected with National Socialism or whether it logically leads to it, abstracted from a private individual's personal reactions, whether happy or unhappy, right or wrong, coherent or incoherent, heroic, cowardly, or criminal."

11. The publication in Germany of the *Introduction to Metaphysics*, the lectures of 1935 in which there appears the famous phrase "the inner truth and greatness" of the National Socialist movement, gave rise in 1953 to a fight in the press between Charles Lewalter (who defended Heidegger and had his support) and a young student from Frankfurt named Jürgen Habermas.

12. Jean Pierre Faye, "Heidegger et la 'révolution,'" *Médiations* 3 (1961).

13. This was the time when Heidegger's life was studied by Paul Hühnerfeld (*In Sachen Heidegger: Versuch über ein deutsches Genie* [1959]) and especially Guido Schneeberger (no-

tably *Nachlese zu Heidegger: Dokumente zu seinem Leben und Denken*, [Berne: Suhr, 1962]).

14. François Fédier, "Trois attaques contre Heidegger," *Critique* 12, no. 234 (October 1966); the discussion concerns Hühnerfeld, Schneeberger, and Theodor Adorno's *The Jargon of Authenticity*, trans. Knut Tarnowski and Frederic Will (Evanston, Ill.: Northwestern University Press, 1973).

15. Faye, "La lecture et l'énoncé," *Critique*, 237 (February 1967).

16. François Fédier, "A propos de Heidegger, une lecture dénoncée," *Critique* 242 (July 1967).

17. Faye's contribution stems from the work he was then doing on Nazi discourse, which was published in 1972: *Langages totalitaires* and *Théorie du récit* (Paris: Hermann).

18. See the article by Hugo Ott, *Neue Zürcher Zeitung* 275 (27 November 1987) to which we will return in chapter 1.

19. Thus, in *La Défaite de la pensée: essai* (Paris: Gallimard, 1987), Alain Finkielkraut explicitly bases his questioning of the "dissolution of culture" on Heidegger's critique of technology: "It is instrumental reason or, to use Heidegger's expression, 'calculative thinking' that makes meditative thought (which we here call 'culture') enter the realm of entertainment." (p. 146) The "tyranny of calculative thinking," which "lowers the culture to the level of unproductive expenses," is here referred to what Heidegger called "technology as the highest form of rational consciousness" ("Overcoming Metaphysics," in M. Heidegger, *The End of Philosophy*, trans. Joan Stambaugh (New York: Harper & Row, 1973), p. 99. We shall return in chapter 4 to the deep reasons that, outside of any strategy, seem to us to prompt this new return to Heidegger.

20. The stakes of what has become "the Farias affair" are thus clear: in a certain way, it stems from the opposition between the "thought of the eighties" and the "thought of 1968." The latter is, moreover, not mistaken about it: to believe *le Monde*, for Philippe Lacoue-Labarthe, the "Heidegger-Farias affair" has taken on such proportions in France because some people have seen in it an "unexpected opportunity" to "have done with Heidegger and his problems," by confirming "the verdict, which was to say the least negative, that has been made" against the "thinking of

1968," "allegedly wholly dominated by Heidegger"; similarly, Derrida attributes the importance given Farias's work to the way in which a certain "democratic discourse" in France—realizing "that its force of consensus rests on traditional philosophical axioms" (human rights, the freedom of the subject)—can never overcome its "anxiety" in the face of "a potential for questioning that is stronger in Heidegger than in many others": how better disguise what is "philosophically fragile" in this "let's say social-democratic" discourse than by freeing oneself of the Heideggerian mortgage? (*Le Monde,* 2 September 1988)

Let us be allowed one simple point: it is not we who wrote Farias's book, nor we who invented the considerable stir it caused among the French intelligentsia.

Chapter 1

1. This is what Pierre Bourdieu thought he could do in his article of 1975. We have nothing to add to the objections we expressed in 1978 ("Heidegger en question," reprinted in Luc Ferry and Alain Renaut, *Système et critique, essai sur la critique de la raison dans la pensée contemporaine* [Brussels: Ousia, 1985]) concerning this wholly external criticism.

2. On the recognition of this "remainder," which radically distinguishes our criticism of the various rehashes of the "external criticism," see our "Heidegger en question," *Système et critique,* p. 26ff. (the deconstruction of metaphysics, the ontological difference).

3. François Fédier, "L'Intention de nuire," *le Débat* 48 (January 1988): 136.

4. Pierre Aubenque, "Encore Heidegger et le nazisme," *le Débat* 48 (January 1988): 113–15.

5. Alain Finkielkraut, *l'Express* (29 January 1988).

6. Philippe Lacoue-Labarthe, "Heidegger, les textes en appel," *le Journal littéraire* 2 (December 1987–January 1988): 116. The book would even be triply suspect because of its taste for buildup, its hodgepodge quality, and its refusal really to read Heidegger's writings.

7. Finkielkraut, *l'Express* (29 January 1988). We should recognize that in other respects Finkielkraut, unlike the orthodox

Heideggerians, does not mean to dodge the basic questions. What he mainly deplores is the self-promotional form taken by this debate.

8. We find, for example, a listing of errors, whose carefulness is not to be doubted, in François Fédier's article "L'Intention de nuire," *le Débat* 48 (January 1988): 136ff.

9. Hugo Ott, "Wege und Abwege. Zu Victor Farias'kritischer Heidegger-Studie," *Neue Zürcher Zeitung* (4 November 1987). Ott is known for his research on Heidegger's involvement with the Nazis: see notably "Martin Heidegger als Rektor der Universität Freiburg i. Br. 1933–1934," *Zeitschrift des Breisgau-Geschichtsvereins* 102 (1983): 121–36 and 103 (1984): 107–30; "Der junge Martin Heidegger Gymnasial-Konviktszeit und Studium," *Freiburger Diozesan-Archiv* (1984): 315–25; "Martin Heidegger als Rektor des Universität Freiburg 1933/34," *Zeitschrift für die Geschichte des Oberrheins* 132 (new series, vol. 93, 1984): 343–58; "Martin Heidegger und die Universität Freiburg nach 1945," *Historisches Jahrbuch* 105, no. 1 (1985): 95–128; "Martin Heidegger und die Nationalsozialismus," in *Heidegger und die praktische Philosophie* (Frankfurt: 1988), pp. 64–77.

10. Gérard Granel, "La guerre de sécession," *le Débat* 48 (January 1988): 142.

11. Ott judges it necessary to "insist on the hitherto inaccessible sources that Farias was able to use," particularly the state archives of the German Democratic Republic, and he notes the contributions of these new facts.

12. Lacoue-Labarthe, "Heidegger, les textes en appel," p. 116.

13. André Glucksmann, *The Master Thinkers*, trans. Brian Pearce (New York: Harper & Row, 1980), p. 94.

14. François Fédier, "L'Intention de nuire," p. 138.

15. Philippe Lacoue-Labarthe, *La Fiction du politique: Heidegger, l'art, la politique* (Paris: Christian Bourgois, 1987), p. 24. Also see p. 34: if we ask what in Nazism was "unacceptable" to Heidegger, "it is obviously, whatever we could say, anti-Semitism."

16. Elisabeth de Fontenay, "Fribourg-Prague-Paris. Comme l'être, la détresse se dit de manières multiples," *le Messager européen* 1 (1987): 94.

17. How could it have been otherwise inasmuch as this racial

biologism meant to give a supposedly scientific foundation for a politics and when, as we all know, for Heidegger science does not lead to "the truth of what is."

18. Here, we set aside all the long-alleged facts condemning the ambiguity in Heidegger's attitude about the "Jewish question": his relations with Husserl, his attitude toward Cassirer, his issuing in 1933 of a decree depriving of every benefit the Jewish students whose fathers were veterans of the First World War, and so on. These facts or evidence are disturbing, but counterbalanced by others, they may not be decisive.

19. This is the claim upheld by Lacoue-Labarthe in *La Fiction du politique*, p. 34. From this suspicion of "blindness," he infers a serious criticism of Heidegger: that of thinking that "the movement's triumph was definitely worth a touch of racism: anti-Semitism was charged to the balance of profits and losses." On this point see also the finely measured observations of Maurice Blanchot, who judges that "a kind of anti-Semitism" could not be wholly alien to someone who belonged to the party in 1933, kept his confidence in Hitler in 1936, and never "agreed to express himself on the Holocaust" (*Critical Inquiry* 15 [Winter 1989]: 478).

20. Victor Farias, *Heidegger and Nazism*, p. 229.

21. Ibid., pp. 208–9.

22. Ibid., pp. 209–11. Pierre Aubenque, "Encore Heidegger et le nazisme," p. 116, note 2, points out that this fact had been known since Karl Jaspers's *Notizen zu Martin Heidegger*, ed. Hans Saner (Munich: Piper, 1978). For all that, Farias's book is quite ambiguous about the date of this letter. "[A]lthough Dr. Vogel put the letter aside in 1933, the case was reopened by his successor," and sent to the minister of education in Berlin (pp. 210–11). Under these circumstances, what is the use of writing: "It should be explained that [the report] is dated 1933 and not 1935, as M. Farias would have us believe." No doubt it is on the basis of such moves as these that one is justified in expressing "doubts about the writer's objectivity, and even his honesty." On the Baumgarten report, see also Lacoue-Labarthe, *La Fiction du politique*, p. 39.

23. François Fédier, *le Nouvel Observateur* (22 January 1988): 84.

24. André Boutot, author of *Heidegger et Platon* (Paris:

Presses Universitaires de France, 1987), *le Monde* (30 October 1987). Similarly, Pierre Aubenque, "Encore Heidegger et le nazisme," p. 113: "Farias contributes little that is truly new."

25. Jacques Derrida, *le Nouvel Observateur* (6–12 November 1987). Lacoue-Labarthe, "Heidegger: les textes en appel," p. 115: "One knew (the best-informed knew) . . ." Along the same lines, Michel Deguy ("Le sozi de Heidegger," *le Débat* [January 1988]) writes: 131: "As J. Derrida has stated . . . most if not all the facts were established and disputed, known and disputed, from the time of Guido Schneeberger and many others."

26. H. Crétella, *le Monde* (30 October 1987).

27. Boutot, *le Monde* (30 October 1987).

28. Without wishing, we repeat, to play the game of "defending" Farias against the Heideggerians, we must still recall that up to now no comparable historical study has ever appeared in French: scattered throughout many articles, the writings of Hugo Ott are untranslated; the study of Bourdieu in 1975 ("Heidegger, un professeur ordinaire," *Actes* 5–6), took no account of the facts, but merely, as usual, the context; as for the studies of the Derridians, they do not provide additional documentary support and are written in a style that restricts them to a privileged public of teachers of philosophy; whatever their merits, articles in specialized journals can never have the influence of a book.

29. How was it with Beaufret himself? Owing to the publication of the letters he wrote in 1978 and 1979 to Robert Faurisson in support of the latter's "revisionist" crusade, it seems that Beaufret had long been aware of the actual duration of Heidegger's Nazi involvement.

30. See Heidegger's description of the scene in the *Spiegel* interview: "To be sure, I did follow the political events of January–March 1933, and also spoke about them from time to time with younger colleagues. My own work, however, was concerned with a more comprehensive interpretation of pre-Socratic thought." (" 'Only a God Can Save Us': The *Spiegel* Interview," trans. William T. Richardson, in *Heidegger: The Man and the Thinker*, ed. Thomas Sheehan [Chicago: Precedent, 1981], p. 46) Farias establishes that in fact Heidegger's accession to the rectorate was a direct part of the Nazi Party's strategy for establishing, with the help of student organizations, its power in the Baden area.

31. Heidegger, "Call to the students at Freiburg on the occa-

sion of the plebiscite scheduled for 12 November 1933." Cited in Farias, *Heidegger and Nazism*, p. 118.

32. See, for example, the 1945 "The Rectorate 1933/1934: Facts and Thoughts," which was given by Heidegger to his son and only published in 1983 (Frankfurt: Klostermann), which says: "In this manner I hoped to counter the advance of unsuited persons and the threatening hegemony of the party apparatus and party doctrine." (trans. Karsten Harries, *Review of Metaphysics* 38 [March 1985]: 484).

33. Concerning this goal and the means Heidegger envisioned, see the plan written in September 1934, *after his resignation from the rectorate,* for the Academy of Professors of the German Reich (quoted by Farias, p. 198): to train professors capable of actualizing the future university, we must "rethink traditional *science* in terms of the strengths of National Socialism."

34. We leave aside here the purely interpretive side of Farias's book. We say merely that its main hypothesis (for all that, it seems, completely new)—to wit, that Heidegger identified himself with the populist and radically "revolutionary" SA wing of the Nazi Party and that his (relative) withdrawal in 1934 was a reflection of the defeat within the Party of Ernst Röhm and his followers—seems brilliant. Heidegger remained a party member, scrupulously paying his dues until the end of the war, but after the Night of the Long Knives (30 June 1934) he belonged to the camp of the vanquished. "The Rectorate" (p. 499) is almost explicit in this regard: "About the possible consequences of my resignation from office in the spring of 1934 I had few illusions; after June 30 of that year I had none. Anyone who after that assumed a leadership function in the university could know beyond the shadow of a doubt with whom he was dealing."

Chapter 2

1. Jean Beaufret, *Entretien avec Frédéric de Towarnicki* (Paris: Presses Universitaires de France, 1984), p. 87.

2. See Alain Renaut, "Qu'est-ce que l'homme? Essais sur le chemin de pensée de Heidegger," *Man and World* 9, no. 1 (1976).

The next few pages repeat, with merely some formal changes, the interpretation he proposed twelve years ago.

3. Martin Heidegger, *Being and Time* (1927), trans. John Macquarrie and Edward Robinson (New York: Harper & Row, 1962), p. 43; *Sein und Zeit* (Halle: Niemeyer, 1927), p. 21.

4. Ibid., p. 60 (*Sein und Zeit,* p. 36).

5. Ibid., p. 133 (p. 100).

6. Ibid., p. 168 (p. 130).

7. See also § 43, pp. 245–46 (p. 201).

8. Ibid., p. 250 (p. 206).

9. Ibid., p. 166 (p. 128).

10. Ibid., p. 223 (p. 179).

11. Ibid., p. 224 (p. 179).

12. Ibid., p. 172 (p. 134).

13. Ibid., pp. 166, 183–84, 219–20 (pp. 128, 144, 175).

14. Ibid., pp. 167, 237 (pp. 129, 193).

15. Ibid., p. 167 (p. 129).

16. Ibid., pp. 232, 233 (pp. 187, 189).

17. Ibid., p. 268 (p. 225).

18. Ibid., p. 311 (p. 267).

19. Farias, *Heidegger and Nazism,* p. 118.

20. Martin Heidegger, "The Self-Assertion of the German University: Address, delivered on the Solemn Assumption of the Rectorate of the University of Freiburg," trans. Karsten Harries, *Review of Metaphysics* 38 (March 1985): 479–80.

21. Martin Heidegger, in Schneeberger, *Nachlese,* no. 114.

22. Similarly (Schneeberger, no. 132): "It is a new start for a revivified youth that believes in its recovered roots."

23. Ibid.

24. Farias, *Heidegger and Nazism,* p. 119.

25. Renaut, "Qu'est-ce que l'homme?" p. 19.

26. Quoted by Farias, *Heidegger and Nazism,* pp. 138–39.

27. Louis Althusser, "Response to John Lewis," in *Essays in Self-criticism,* trans. Graham Lodge (Atlantic Highlands, NJ: Humanities Press, 1976).

28. Alain Finkielkraut, *l'Express* (29 January 1988).

29. Here we mean the interpretation proposed by Derrida himself, before Farias's book appeared, in *On Spirit: Heidegger and the Question,* trans. Geoffrey Bennington and Rachel

Bowlby (Chicago: University of Chicago Press, 1989) (and later discussed by him in connection with the public reception of the book [le Nouvel Observateur (6–12 November 1987)]); and also the remarks of Elisabeth de Fontenay, "Fribourg-Prague-Paris. Comme l'être, la détresse se dit de manières multiples," le Messager européen 1 (1987), and Philippe Lacoue-Labarthe, La Fiction du politique: Heidegger, l'art et la politique (Strasbourg: 1987), which in its original form was also published before Heidegger et Nazisme, but was later expanded (in the Bourgois edition of February 1988) with a short discussion of Farias's claims. Obviously by calling them "Derridian" we are not describing these interpretations but merely giving them their common denominator.

30. Le Débat 48 (January 1988): 120. See also Michel Deguy, "Le sozi de Heidegger," le Débat 48 (January 1988): 131; Gérard Granel, le Débat 48 (January 1988): 145; and even Stephan Moses, le Débat 48 (January 1988): 170: "The work that Jacques Derrida has just devoted to the erratic byways of some Heideggerian themes (spirit, the hand) indicates the path we should follow to determine how certain central aspects of this philosophy could degenerate to the point of joining up with the themes of the Nazi ideology."

31. Heidegger, Being and Time, p. 72 (p. 46).

32. Ibid., §77.

33. See Derrida, Of Spirit, p. 49ff. (on §82).

34. Heidegger, "Self-Assertion of the German University," p. 474.

35. Derrida, Of Spirit, p. 32.

36. Ibid., p. 39.

37. Ibid.

38. Ibid.

39. Ibid.: "By the same token, this sets apart [démarque] Heidegger's commitment and breaks an affiliation."

40. Ibid., p. 45.

41. Using a procedure all his own, Derrida takes pains to suggest how even in this final idea of the spirit, Heidegger may have been unable to avoid all the dangers of his earlier moves (p. 100ff.). At least he indicates a way, in which of course it is up to each person to go even further than Heidegger in the direction of

what he uncovered. And on this way, happily, Derrida has arrived.

42. Ibid., pp. 39–40.

43. Ibid., p. 56.

44. Ibid., p. 120.

45. From an interview published in *le Nouvel Observateur* 9 (6 November 1987).

46. de Fontenay, "Fribourg-Prague-Paris," pp. 114, 89, 93, 98.

47. Lacoue-Labarthe, *la Fiction du politique*, pp. 44, 61, 66, 80–81. It stands to reason—and this is equally true of Elisabeth de Fontenay's article—that, although the end point is exactly the same as Derrida's, the deployment of the analysis is not unoriginal nor without nuances in relation to the interrogation developed in *Of Spirit*.

48. *Le Nouvel Observateur* (27 November 1987).

Chapter 3

1. Martin Heidegger, *Introduction to Metaphysics* (1935), trans. Ralph Manheim (New Haven: Yale University Press, 1959), p. 199. Concerning his retention in 1952 of this sentence from 1935, see Heidegger's explanation in "Only a God Can Save Us," pp. 45–67.

2. Ibid.

3. Heidegger, "Only a God Can Save Us," p. 55.

4. Ibid.

5. Heidegger, *Nietzsche*, trans. David Farrell Krell (New York: Harper & Row, 1977).

6. Heidegger, "The Onto-theological Constitution of Metaphysics," in *Identity and Difference*, trans. Joan Stambaugh (New York: Harper & Row, 1969), p. 5.

7. Heidegger, "The Age of the World Picture," in *The Question Concerning Technology, and Other Essays*, trans. William Lovitt (New York: Garland, 1977), p. 116.

8. Heidegger, *Being and Time*, trans. John Macquarrie and Edward Robinson (New York: Harper & Row, 1962), p. 100; *Sein und Zeit* (Halle: Niemeyer, 1927), p. 70.

9. Heidegger, "The Question Concerning Technology,"

trans. William Lovitt, in *Heidegger, Basic Writings*, ed. David Farrell Krell (New York: Harper & Row, 1977), p. 297.

10. Heidegger, "Memorial Address," in *Discourse on Thinking*, trans. John M. Anderson and E. Hans Freund (New York: Harper & Row, 1966), p. 49.

11. Heidegger, "What Is Metaphysics?" in *Heidegger: Basic Writings*.

12. Heidegger, *Der Satz vom Grund* (Tübingen: Neske, 1978), p. 66.

13. Heidegger, "Overcoming Metaphysics," in *The End of Philosophy*, trans. Joan Stambaugh (New York: Harper & Row, 1973), p. 104.

14. Heidegger, *Der Satz vom Grund*, p. 138.

15. Heidegger, "What Are Poets For?" in *Poetry, Language, Thought*, trans. Albert Hofstadter (New York: Harper & Row, 1971), p. 116.

16. Heidegger, "Overcoming Metaphysics," p. 93.

17. Ibid., p. 101.

18. Ibid.

19. Ibid., p. 93.

20. Ibid., p. 95.

21. Ibid., p. 90.

22. Having said this, we note that the rapprochement with Max Horkheimer, the one in the 1930s at any rate, soon reached its limits, for Horkheimer criticized the instrumentalization of reason in the name of an objective reason that Heidegger considered no less than instrumental reason "the most implacable foe of thought."

23. See Alain Finkielkraut, *l'Express* (29 January 1988).

24. Martin Heidegger, "The Self-Assertion of the German University: Address, Delivered on the Solemn Assumption of the Rectorate of the University of Freiburg," trans. Karsten Harries, *Review of Metaphysics* 38 (March 1985): 476, 480.

25. Farias, *Heidegger and Nazism* p. 71. "Instruct us, flames, enlighten us. Show us the road from which one does not return!"

26. Heidegger, in Schneeberger, *Nachlese zu Heidegger*.

27. Heidegger, *Nietzsche* I (Paris: Gallimard), pp. 133–34. [Here retranslated from the French.]

28. Heidegger, "What Are Poets For?" p. 112.

29. Heidegger, "Science and Reflection," in *The Question Concerning Technology, and Other Essays*, p. 167.

30. Heidegger, "Overcoming Metaphysics," p. 105.

31. On this theme, see notably "The Turning," a 1949 lecture appearing in *Question Concerning Technology*, pp. 37–38: "If Enframing is a destining of the coming to presence of Being itself. . . . If the essence, the coming to presence, of technology, Enframing as the danger within Being, is Being itself, then technology will never allow itself to be mastered, either positively or negatively, by a human doing founded merely on itself. Technology, whose essence is Being itself, will never allow itself to be overcome by men."

32. Heidegger, *Introduction to Metaphysics*, p. 37.

33. Yet it is in no way isolated. The lectures on Hölderlin from the summer term of 1942 make "Bolshevism" merely "a variant of Americanism" (*Gesamtausgabe*, vol. 53, p. 86). The same thing appears again in his "Only a God Can Save Us," p. 55.

34. Martin Heidegger, *Heraclit* (1943), *Gesamtausgabe*, vol. 55 (1979), p. 123. (trans. Thomas Sheehan, "Heidegger and the Nazis," *New York Review of Books* [16 June 1988]: 45) Nicolas Tertullian quotes this passage in a relevant article on Heidegger's references to Nazism in his lectures after his resignation from the rectorate (*Quinzaine littéraire* [15–31 December 1987]).

35. Heidegger, "Age of the World Picture," pp. 132–33.

36. Heidegger, "Only a God Can Save Us," p. 55.

37. Ibid., p. 61.

38. Heidegger, "What Are Poets For?" p. 113. In this sense, stresses Heidegger, "Americanism is something European" (ibid., p. 153). The term comes from Rilke, whose *Letters to Muzot* Heidegger quotes: "Now there are intruding, from America, empty and indifferent things, sham things, the trompe-l'oeils of life. . . . A house, as the Americans understand it, an American apple or a wine stock from over there have *nothing* in common with the house, the fruit, the grapes into which the hope and thoughtfulness of our forebears had entered. . . ." (ibid., p. 113).

39. Finkielkraut, *l'Express* (29 January 1988).

40. Maurice Blanchot strongly emphasizes this point in "Thinking the Apocalypse: A Letter from Maurice Blanchot to

Catherine David," trans. Paula Wissing, *Critical Inquiry* 15
(Winter 1989): 475–80.

41. Heidegger, "Only a God Can Save Us," p. 55.
42. Ibid., p. 56.
43. Heidegger, "Overcoming Metaphysics," p. 108.
44. Heidegger, "Only a God Can Save Us," p. 57.
45. Ibid., pp. 61, 60.
46. Heidegger, "Self-Assertion of the German University," p.
474.
47. Heidegger, *"Arbeitdienst und Universität,"* in *Nachlese
zu Heidegger,"* pp. 63ff. See also 12 November 1933: "Work en-
ables the people to win back their rootedness" (ibid., no. 57).
The "Appeal for the Plebiscite of 12 November 1933" hails "the
fresh start of a young people who believe in their recovered
roots" and have freed themselves of "the idolatry of thought be-
reft of soil and power" (ibid., no. 132). Against the uniformitization of an Americanized humanity, "each people [must] find and
preserve the greatness and truth of its determination" (ibid.).
48. Heidegger, "Self-Assertion of the German University," p.
475.
49. Ibid., p. 473.
50. Concerning this text, see Tertullian (*Quinzaine littéraire*
[15–31 December 1987]): Heidegger writes that these manipula-
tions are of no service to "National Socialism and its historical
singularity," a service for which "National Socialism has no
need"; "one renders no service to the knowledge and estimation
of the historical unicity of National Socialism by interpreting
the Greek phenomenon in such a way that one could believe that
the Greeks were already all National Socialists." (*Gesamtausgabe*, vol. 53, pp. 98–106).
51. Quoted in Farias, *Heidegger and Nazism*, p. 135.
52. This fitting of Nazism into the age of technology nevertheless does not uniquely concern its "Hitlerian deviation," for,
as we have seen, "Overcoming Metaphysics" makes the coming
of the führers an inevitable consequence of the technological
"enframing" of the world. In its principle (here the *Führerprinzip*) as well as its reality, Nazism thus was *also* interpreted by
Heidegger, parallel to the antimodern interpretation, as a movement leading modernity beyond itself, notably by submission to
the requirements of technology, beyond democracy.

53. Raymond Aron, *Démocratie et totalitarisme* (Paris: Gallimard, 1965), pp. 232–41.

54. Louis Dumont, *Essays on Individualism* (Chicago: University of Chicago Press, 1986), pp. 149–79: "The Totalitarian Disease: Individualism and Racism in Adolf Hitler's Representations."

55. Heidegger, "The Anaximander Fragment," in *Early Greek Thinking*, trans. David Farrell Krell and Frank A. Capuzzi (New York: Harper & Row, 1975), p. 26.

56. This is the reason why, according to a displacement often noted by the commentators, the act of "overcoming" (*Überwindung*) tends to give way to one of *Verwindung* (remission) that allows the decline to run its course.

57. Concerning this predicament, see Luc Ferry and Alain Renaut, *Système et critique, essai sur la critique de la raison dans la pensée contemporaine* (Brussels: Ousia, 1985), p. 92ff.

58. Heidegger, introduction to "What Is Metaphysics?" trans. Walter Kaufmann, in *Existentialism from Dostoevsky to Sartre*, 2d edition (New York: New American Library, 1975), pp. 268–69.

59. Ibid., p. 269.

60. Ibid.

61. Heidegger, "Only a God Can Save Us," p. 57ff.

62. Ibid., p. 56ff.

63. Heidegger, "Overcoming Metaphysics," p. 102.

64. Heidegger, "Only a God Can Save Us," p. 61.

65. See Ferry and Renaut, "L'Éthique après Heidegger," in *Système et critique*.

66. In a letter of 13 March 1974 to Heinrich Weigand Petzet, Heidegger, endorsing his condemnation of a democratic Europe, quotes J. Burckhardt: "Our Europe is being ruined from below by 'democracy,' in the face of an 'above' that is insufficiently numerous." H. W. Petzet, *Auf einen Stern zugehen* (Frankfurt: Societätsverlag, 1983), p. 231.

Chapter 4

1. On the definition of the concept of democratic individualism as a struggle, possibly collective, of individuals against

hierarchies in the name of equality, and against tradition (heteronomy) in the name of freedom (autonomy), see Luc Ferry and Alain Renaut, 68–86, *Itinéraires de l'individu* (Paris: Gallimard, 1987).

2. Contrary to what might be said here or there, Gilles Lipovetsky's book *l'Empire de l'éphèmère* (Paris: Gallimard, 1987) is in no way an apologia for the frivolous nor a hymn to the glories of consumerism. The impression—in itself inarguable—that *l'Empire de l'éphèmère* is "more optimistic," that *l'Ere du vide* concerns merely the polemical context of Lipovetsky's argument against the dominant ideology according to which mass culture must be a matter of alienation. In this sense, the book's conclusion represents, not a reversal, but Lipovetsky's basic claim: "Fashion is neither angel nor beast; there is also a tragedy of lightness set up as a social system, an inexpungeable tragic side to the scale of the subjective units. The total reign of fashion eases social discord but escalates subjective and intersubjective conflict; it allows greater individual freedom, but fosters a weariness of living. The lesson is hard; the progress of the philosophes and that of happiness march to different drummers; the counterpart of the euphoria of fashion is dereliction, depression, and existential turmoil."

3. Max Horkheimer, "Kritische Theorie heute und gestern," in *Gesellschaft im Übergang* (Frankfurt, 1972).

4. It is interesting to note that, in a rather similar way, Max Weber's thinking could give rise in some people's minds to the myth of an "end of ideologies" owing to a confusion of liberalism and socialism in the ideal type of bureaucracy.

5. Martin Heidegger, *Introduction to Metaphysics*, trans. Ralph Manheim (New Haven: Yale University Press, 1959), pp. 37–38 (emphasis added).

6. See *le Messager européen* 1, p. 317ff.: "The archives of barbarity." [Yves Mourousi is a well-known political newscaster on French television.—Trans.]

7. Philippe Lacoue-Labarthe, *la Fiction du politique: Heidegger, l'art et la politique,* (Paris: Christian Bourgois, 1987), p. 25.

8. Concerning this point, see Robert Legros's excellent book *Le Jeune Hegel et la naissance de la pensée romantique* (Brussels: Ousia, 1980).

9. See Luc Ferry, "Droit, coutume et histoire: Remarques sur Hegel et Savigny," in *la Coutume et la Loi* (Lyons: Presses Universitaires de Lyon, 1986).

10. Joseph de Maistre, *Considerations on France* (1797), trans. Richard A. Lebrun (Montreal: McGill-Queen's University Press, 1974). p. 97.

11. Martin Heidegger, "Letter on Humanism," in *Basic Writings*, ed. David Farrell Krell (New York: Harper & Row, 1977), p. 205.

12. Ibid., p. 206.

13. Ibid., pp. 209ff. We think Heidegger is wrong in reducing existence in Sartre's sense to the *existentia* of metaphysics.

14. Jean-Paul Sartre, *Essays in Existentialism*, ed. Wade Baskin (Secaucus, N. J.: Citadel Press, 1964), p. 34.

15. Ibid., pp. 21–22.

16. Jean Beaufret, *Introduction aux philosophies de l'existence* (Paris: Denoël, 1971), p. 70.

17. Immanuel Kant, *Education*, trans. Annette Churton (Ann Arbor: University of Michigan Press, 1960), pp. 2, 5.

18. Johann Gottlieb Fichte, *The Science of Rights* (1796), trans. A. E. Kroeger [1889] (New York: Harper & Row, 1970), pp. 118–19 (translation modified).

19. See Alexis Philonenko, *La Théorie kantienne de l'histoire* (Paris: Vrin, 1986).

20. Edmund Husserl, "Philosophy and the Crisis of European Humanity," in *The Crisis of European Sciences and Transcendental Phenomenology*, Husserliana, vol. 6, pp. 318ff. (p. 352) (trans. David Carr [Evanston: Northwestern University Press, 1970], pp. 269–99 [p. 273]). Jacques Derrida, *Of Spirit: Heidegger and the Question* (Chicago: University of Chicago Press, 1989), pp. 120–21.

21. On the capacities of criticism to think of action in terms of consciousness and will without falling back into what Heidegger rightly called the metaphysics of subjectivity, see Luc Ferry, *Political Philosophy 2: The System of Philosophies of History*, trans. Franklin Philip (Chicago: University of Chicago Press, forthcoming).

22. See the insightful analyses of Robert Legros, notably in *Etudes phénoménologiques*, nos. 1–2 (Brussels: Ousia, 1985).

Index